Snare Drum Duets

by Ron Spagnardi

Design and Layout by Joe King

CD Engineered by Butch Jones

Published By
Modern Drummer Publications, Inc.
12 Old Bridge Road
Cedar Grove, NJ 07009 USA

Contents

INTRODUCTION

Snare Drum Duets offers a selection of twenty-five challenging duets that range in difficulty from relatively simple to more complex. A wide assortment of time signatures is used throughout the book, from 2/4 and common time to 5/8, 7/8, and 12/8, among others.
  Snare Drum Duets can be used in several different ways:

1) For those working with the book without the benefit of a second player, snare drum parts one and two can be practiced as individual solos for improvement of basic reading skills.

2) Two players may use the book as written in duet format, remembering to alternate parts. The metronome marking above each duet indicates the speed at which the material is performed on the accompanying CD. However, the tempo can be adjusted up or down in accordance with the ability of the players. Obviously, precise execution and perfect timing are essential on the part of both players when performing the material in duet format.

3) Finally, for those studying the material without a playing partner, the enclosed CD includes a separate recording of parts one and two of each duet, thus enabling you to perform either part along with the other on the CD.

  Conscientious practice of the material in *Snare Drum Duets* will most definitely improve both reading and technical skills, regardless of the manner in which the book is utilized. Good luck.

Ron Spagnardi

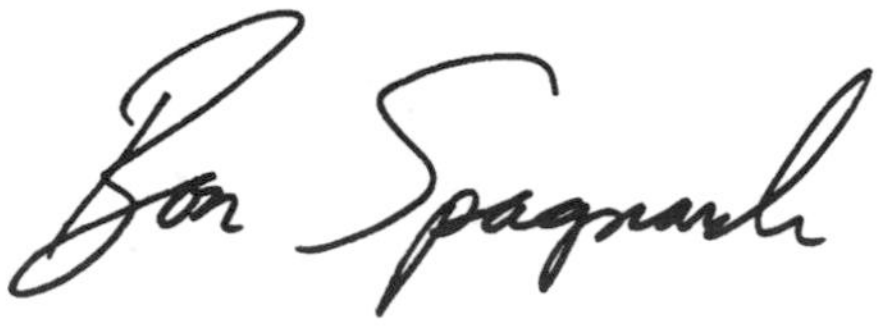

Duet 1

Tracks 1 and 2

♩ =88

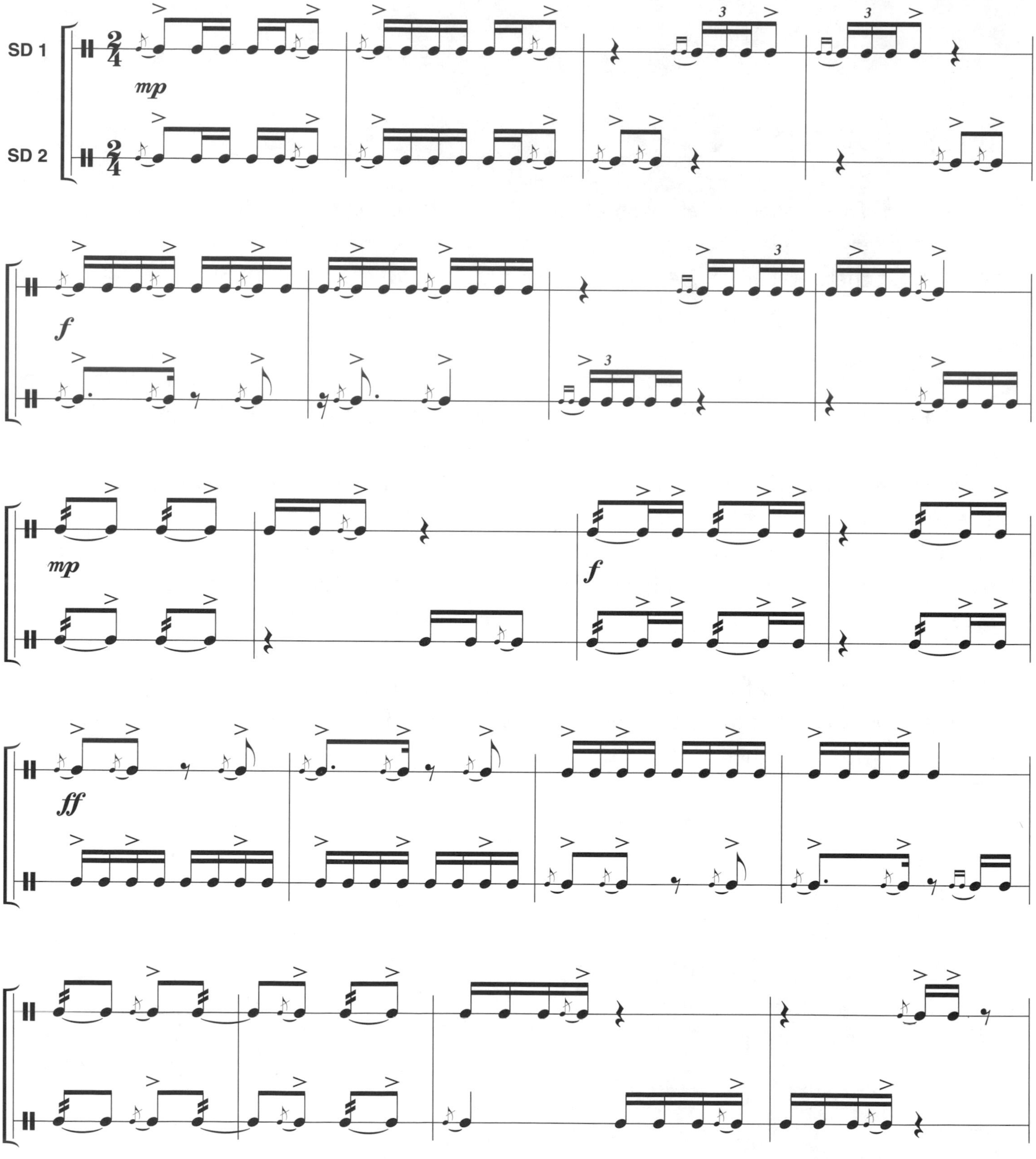

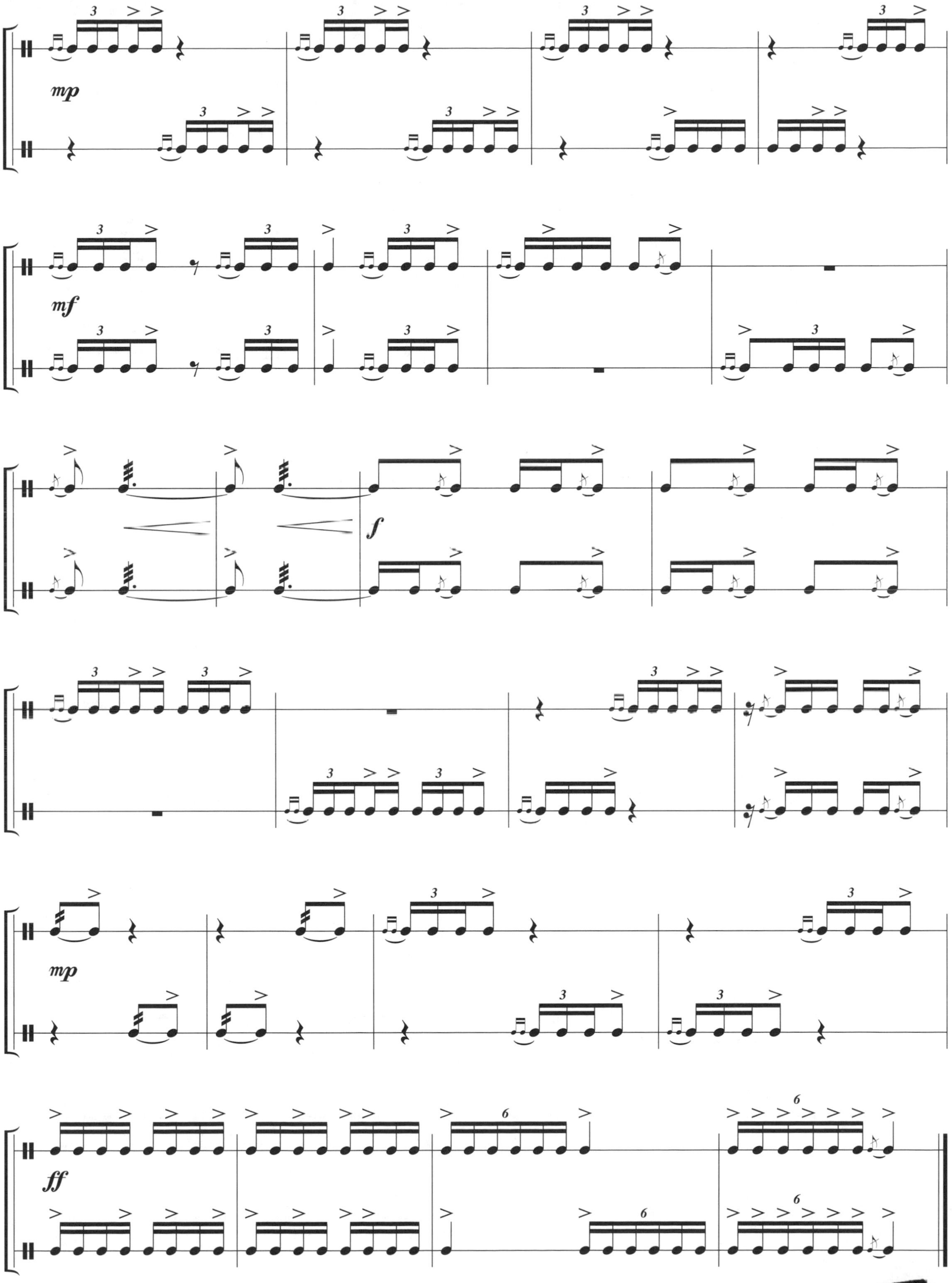
mp
mf
f
mp
ff

Duet 2

Tracks 3 and 4

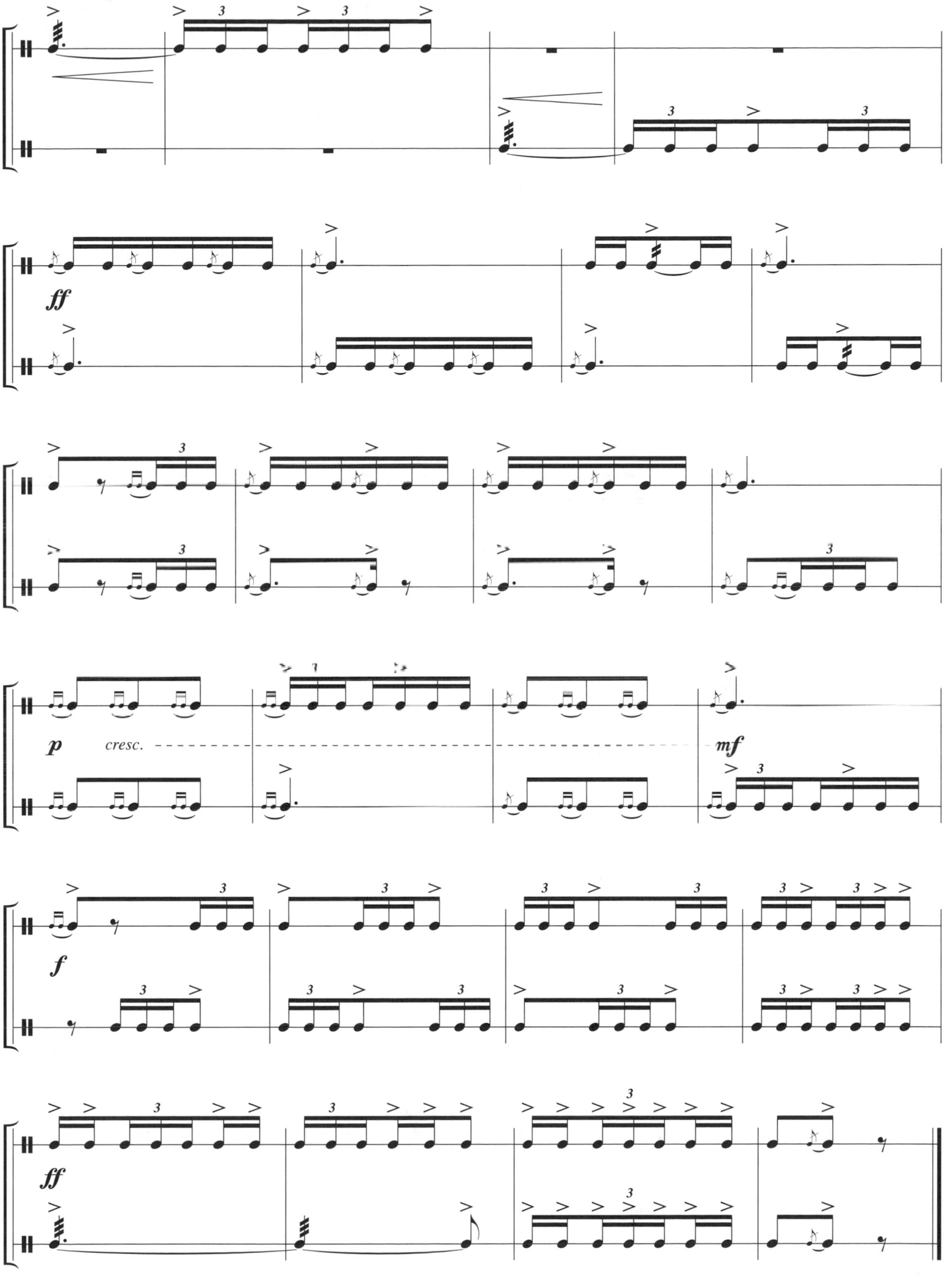
ff
p
cresc.
mf
f
ff

Duet 3

Tracks 5 and 6

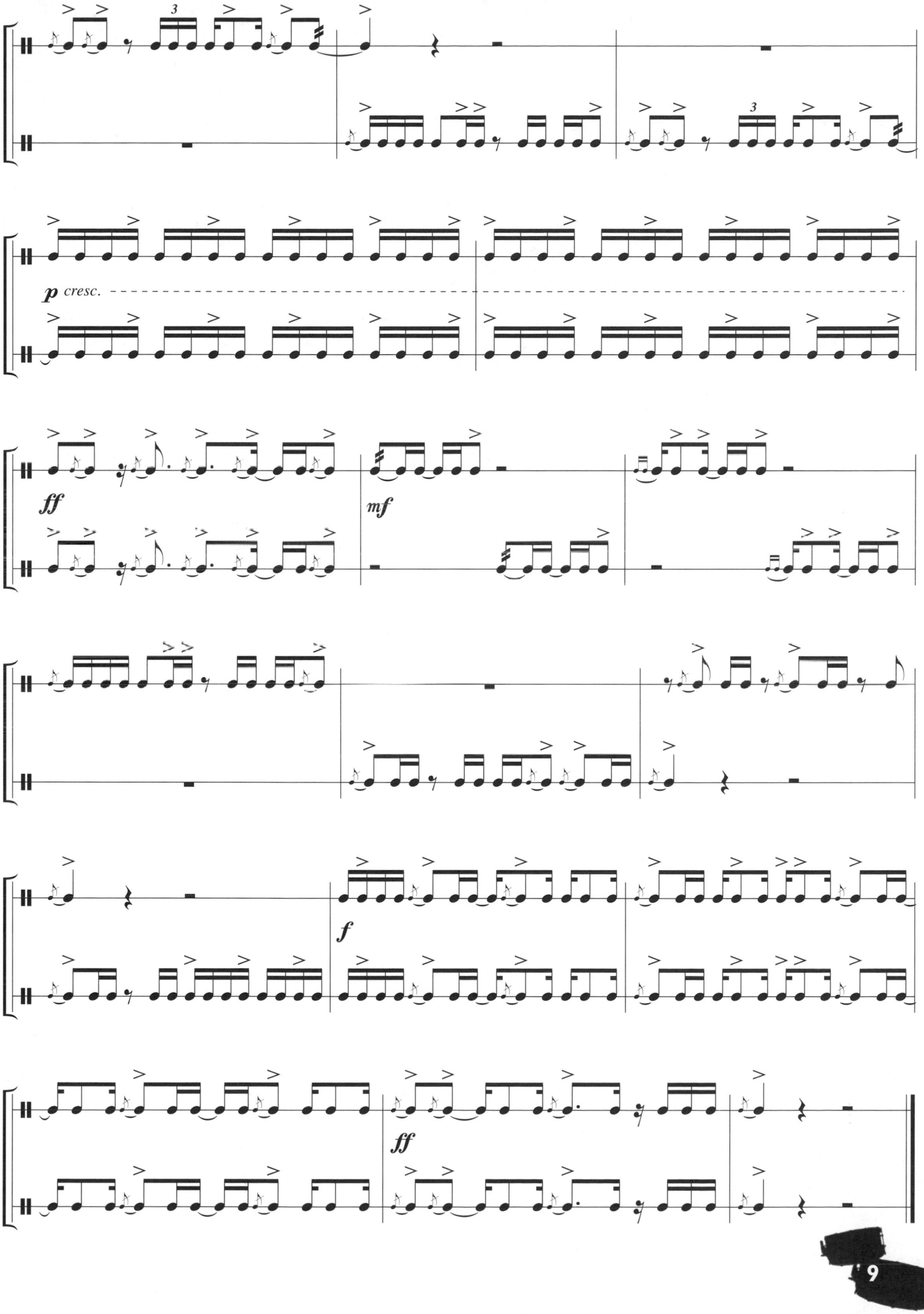
3
p cresc.
ff
mf
f
ff

Duet 4

Tracks 7 and 8

♩=150

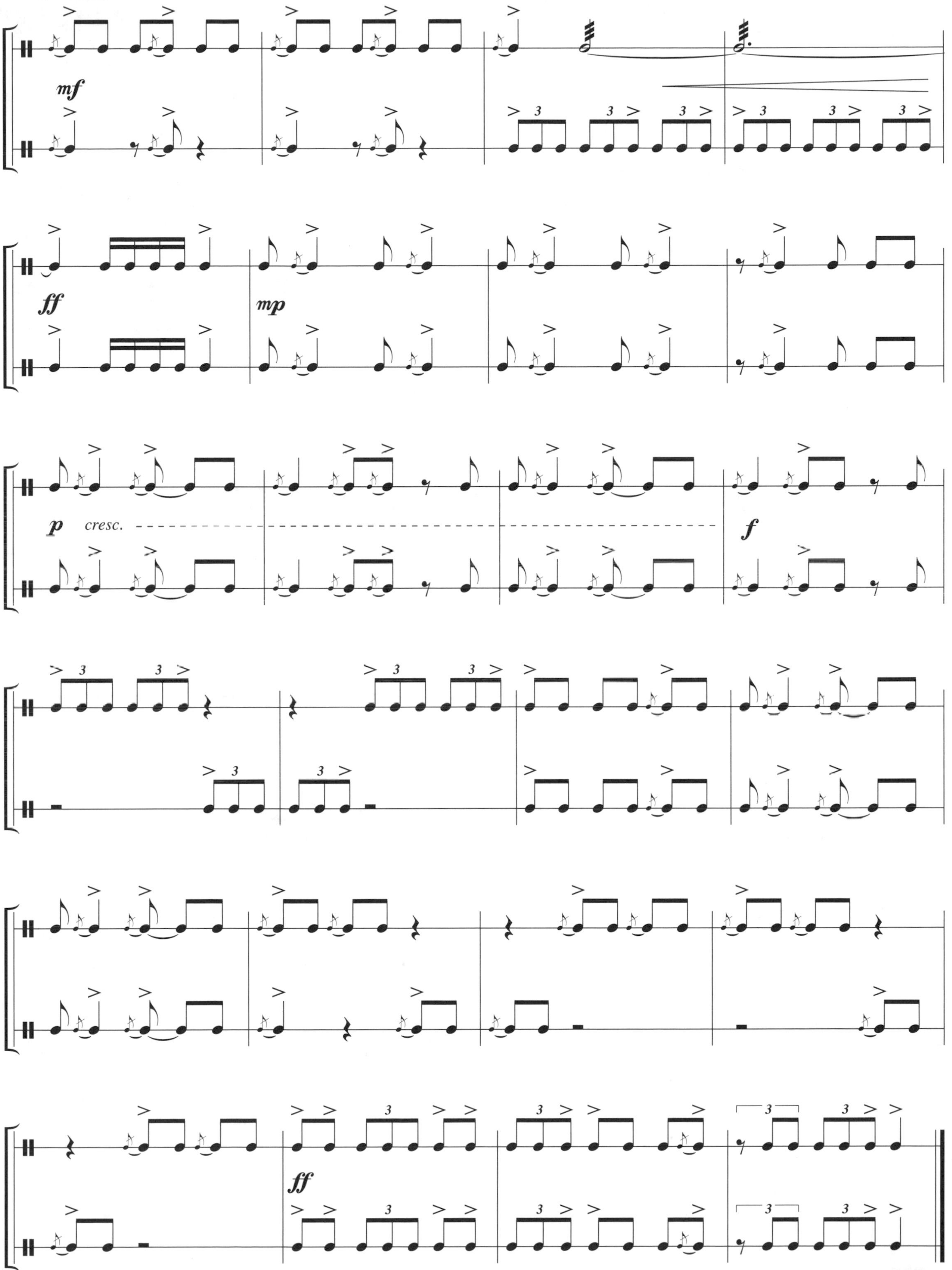
mf
ff
mp
p cresc.
f
ff

Duet 5

Tracks 9 and 10

♩. = 52

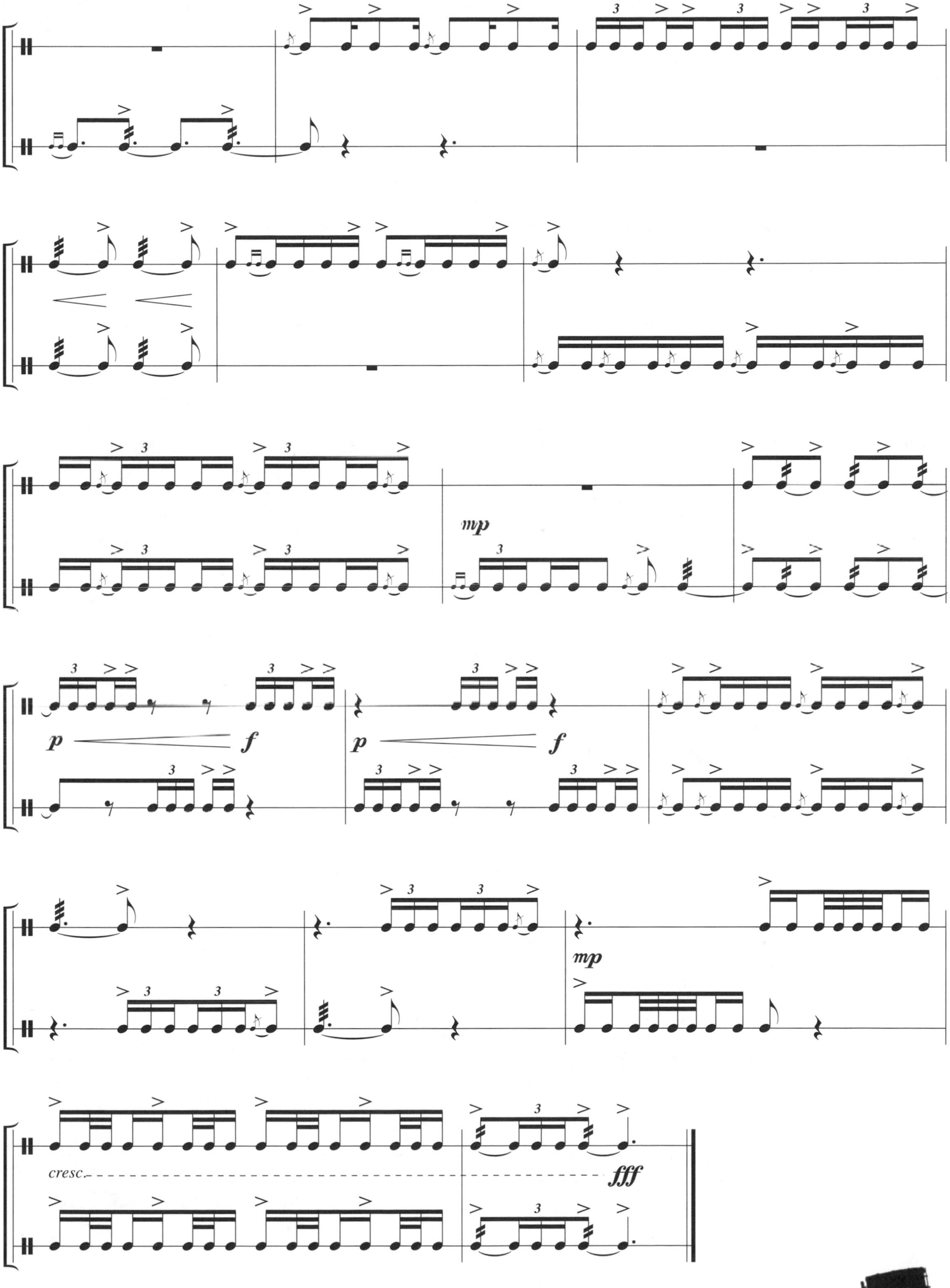
mp
p
f
p
f
mp
cresc.
fff

Duet 6

Tracks 11 and 12

♩=135

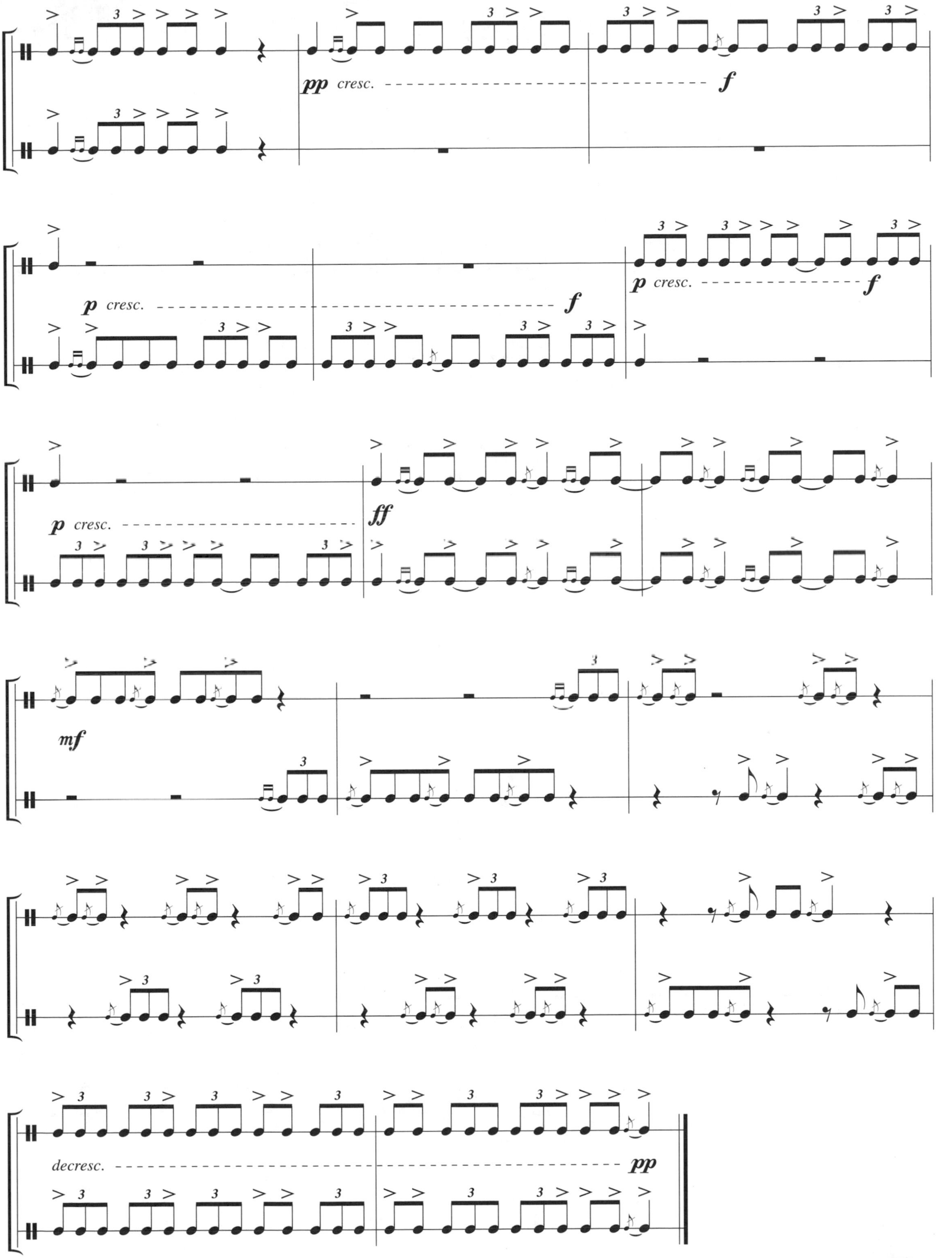
pp cresc.
f
p cresc.
f
p cresc.
f
p cresc.
ff
mf
decresc.
pp

Duet 7

Tracks 13 and 14

♩=78

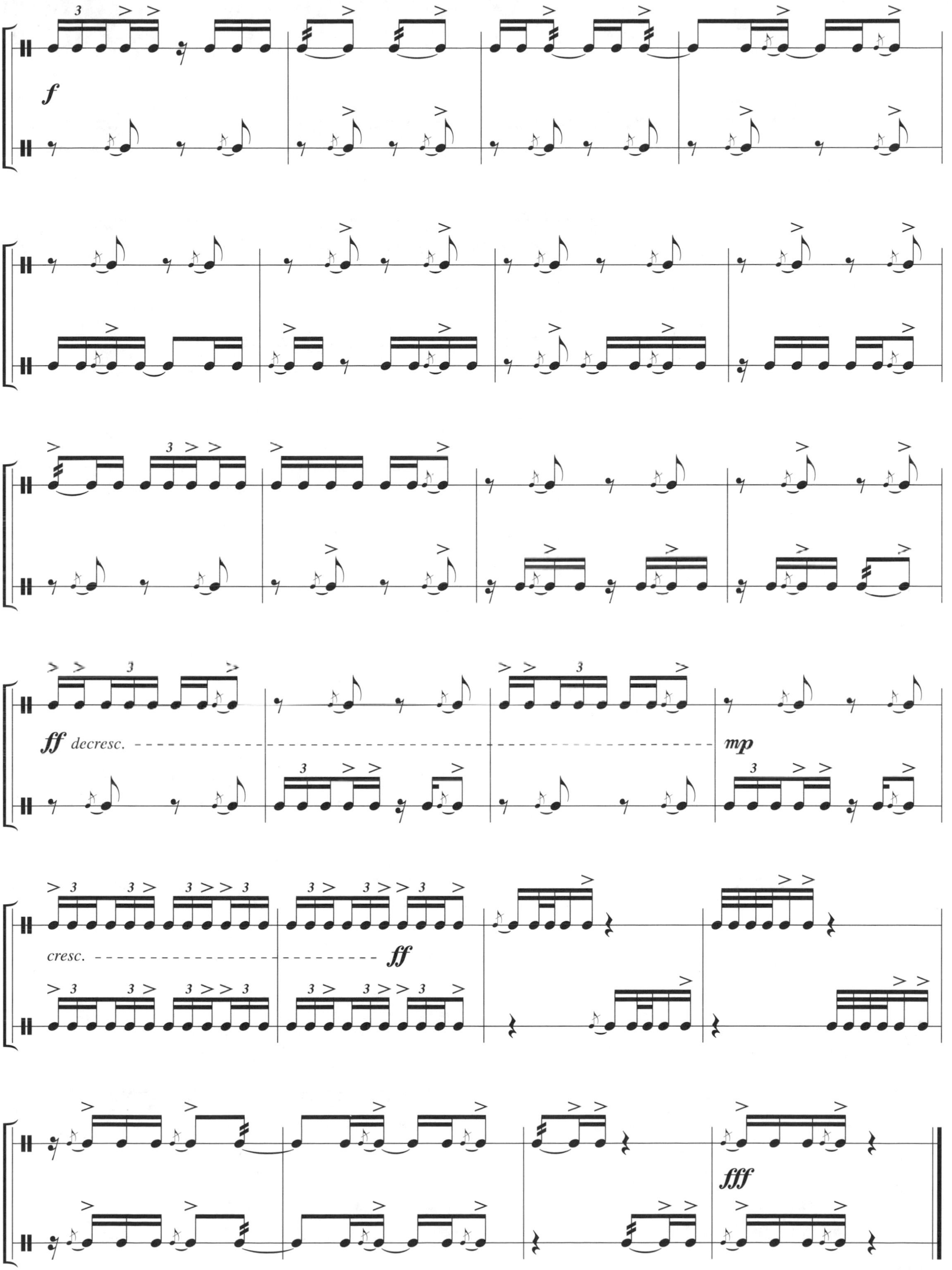
f
ff decresc.
mp
cresc.
ff
fff

Duet 8

Tracks 15 and 16

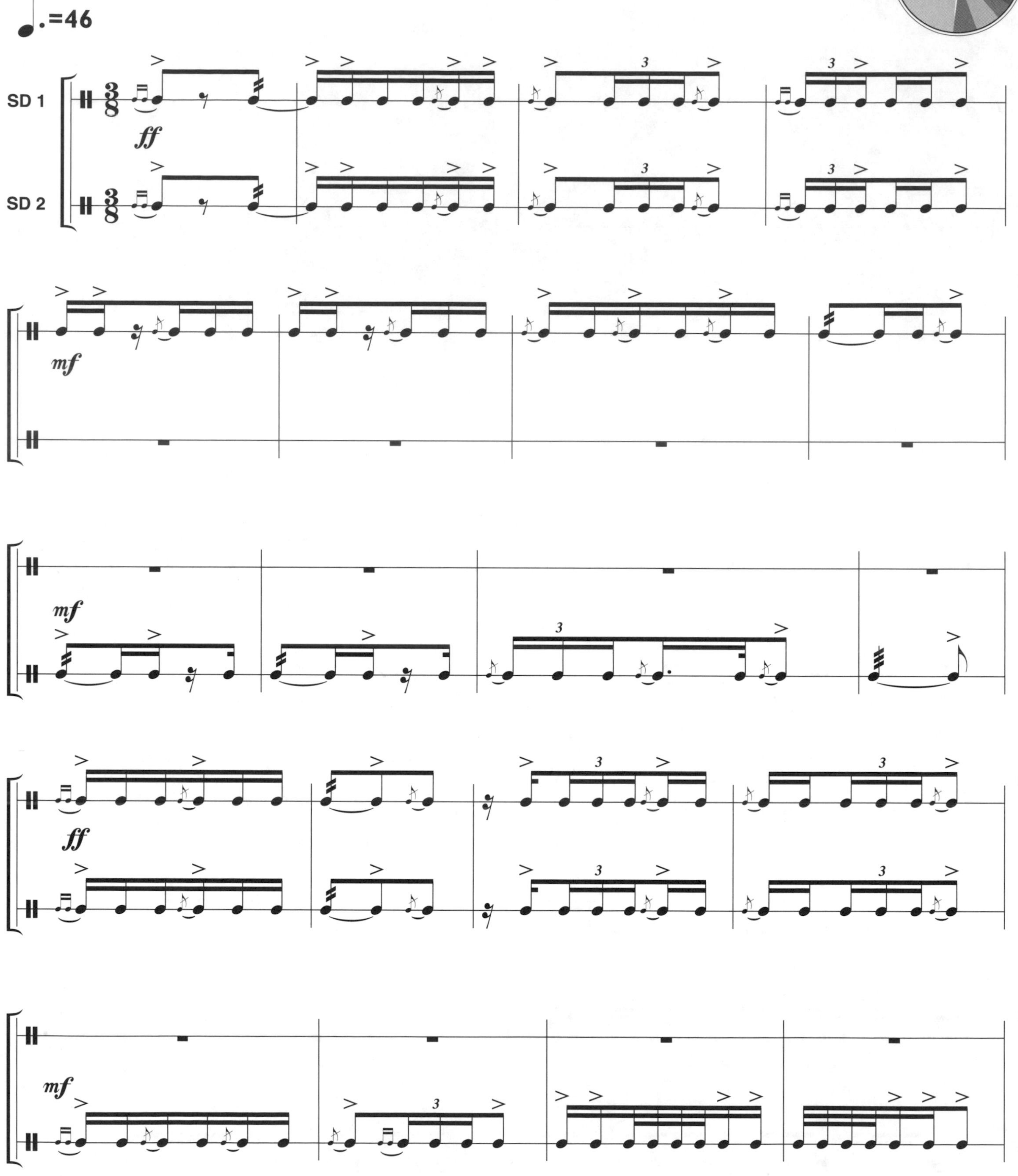

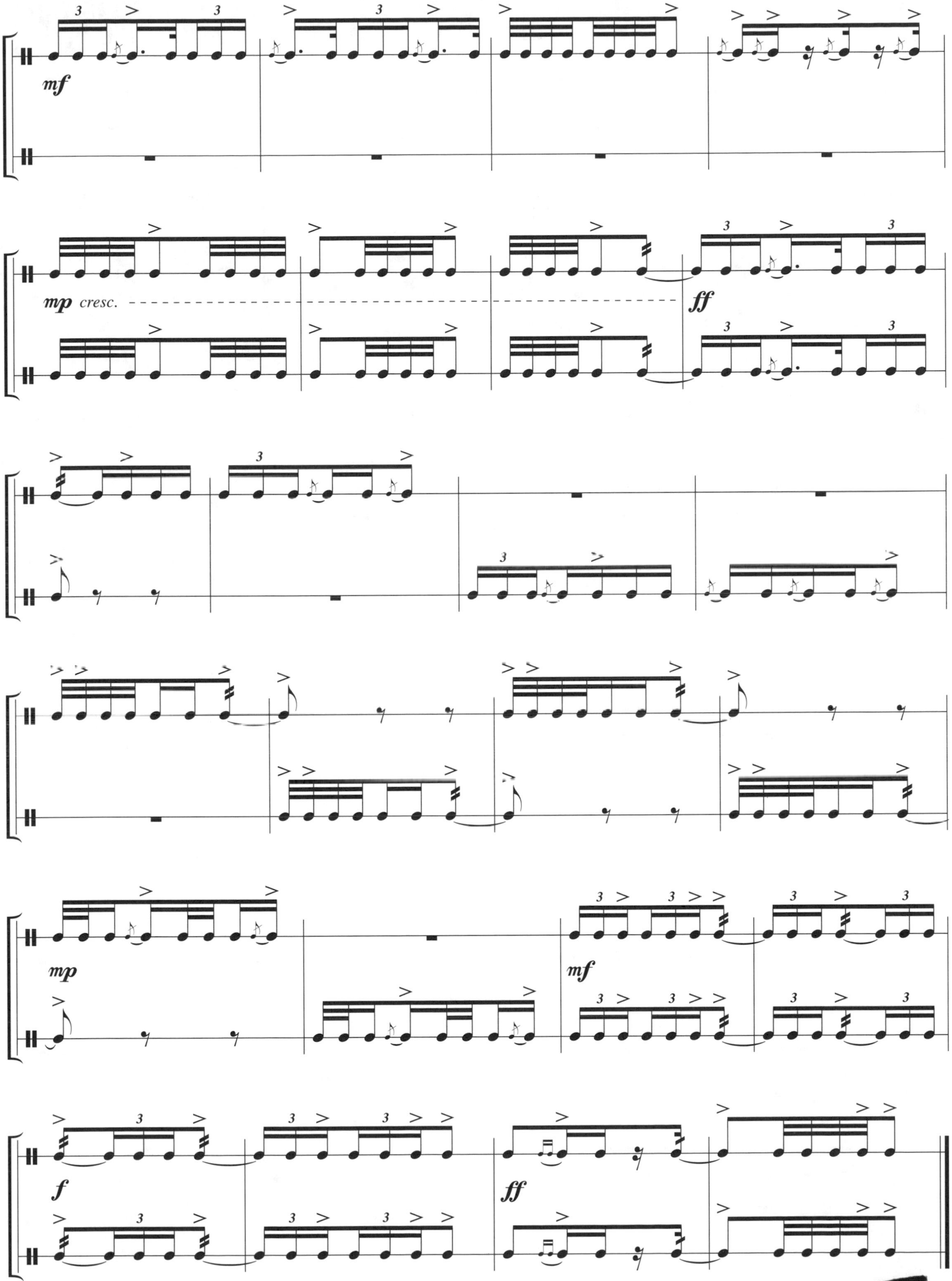
mf
mp cresc.
ff
mp
mf
f
ff

Duet 9

Tracks 17 and 18

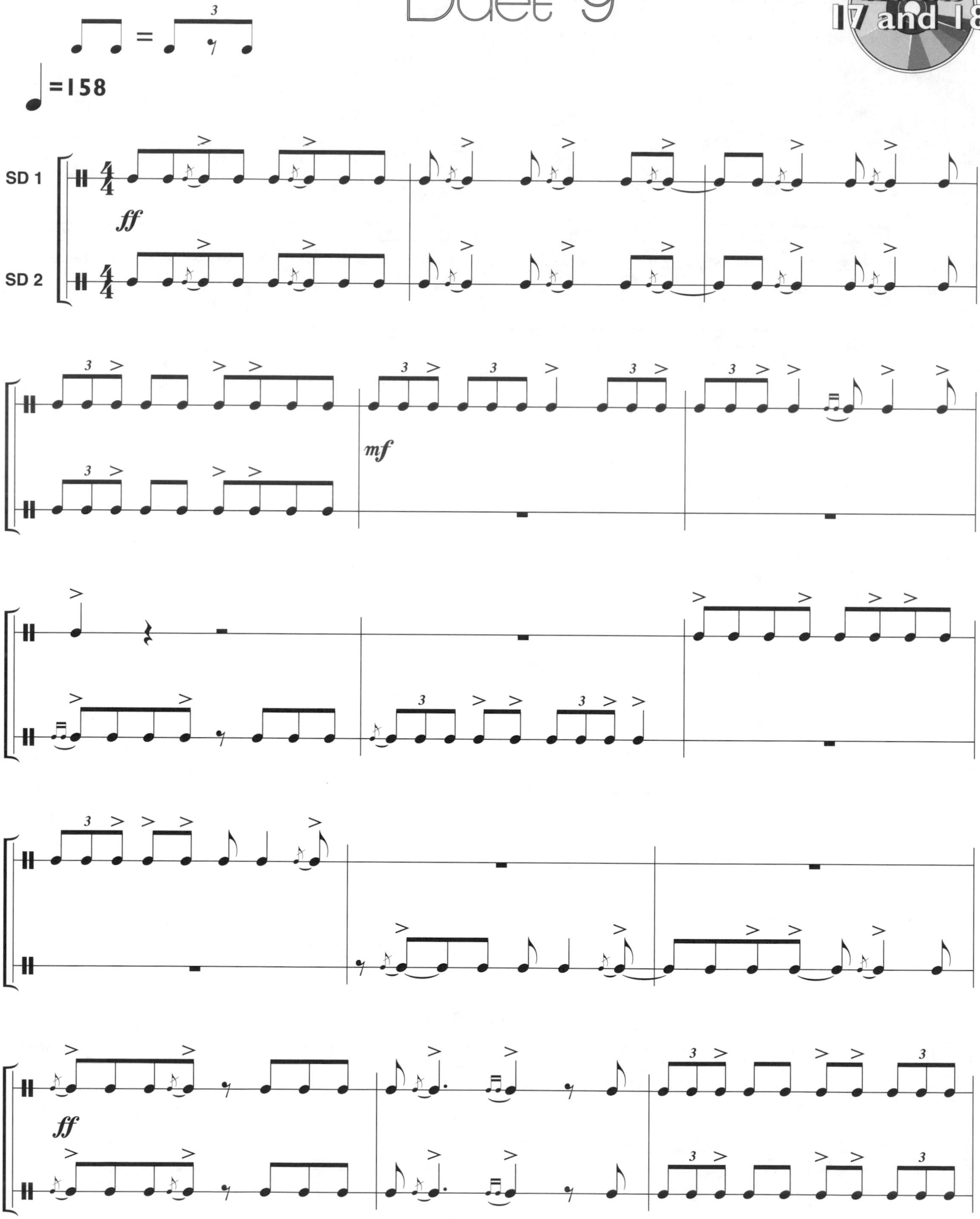

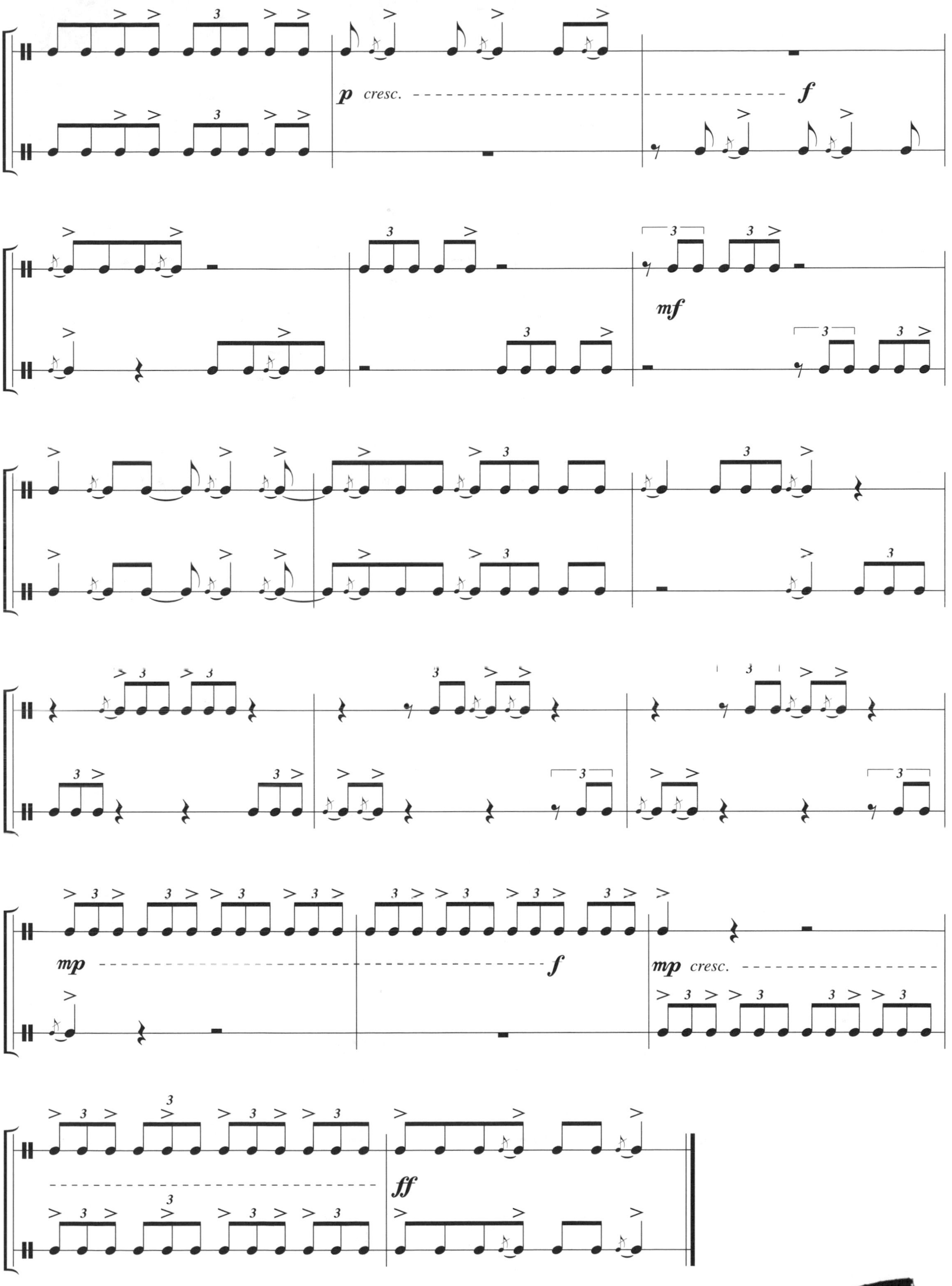
p cresc.
f
mf
mp
f
mp cresc.
ff

Duet 10

Tracks 19 and 20

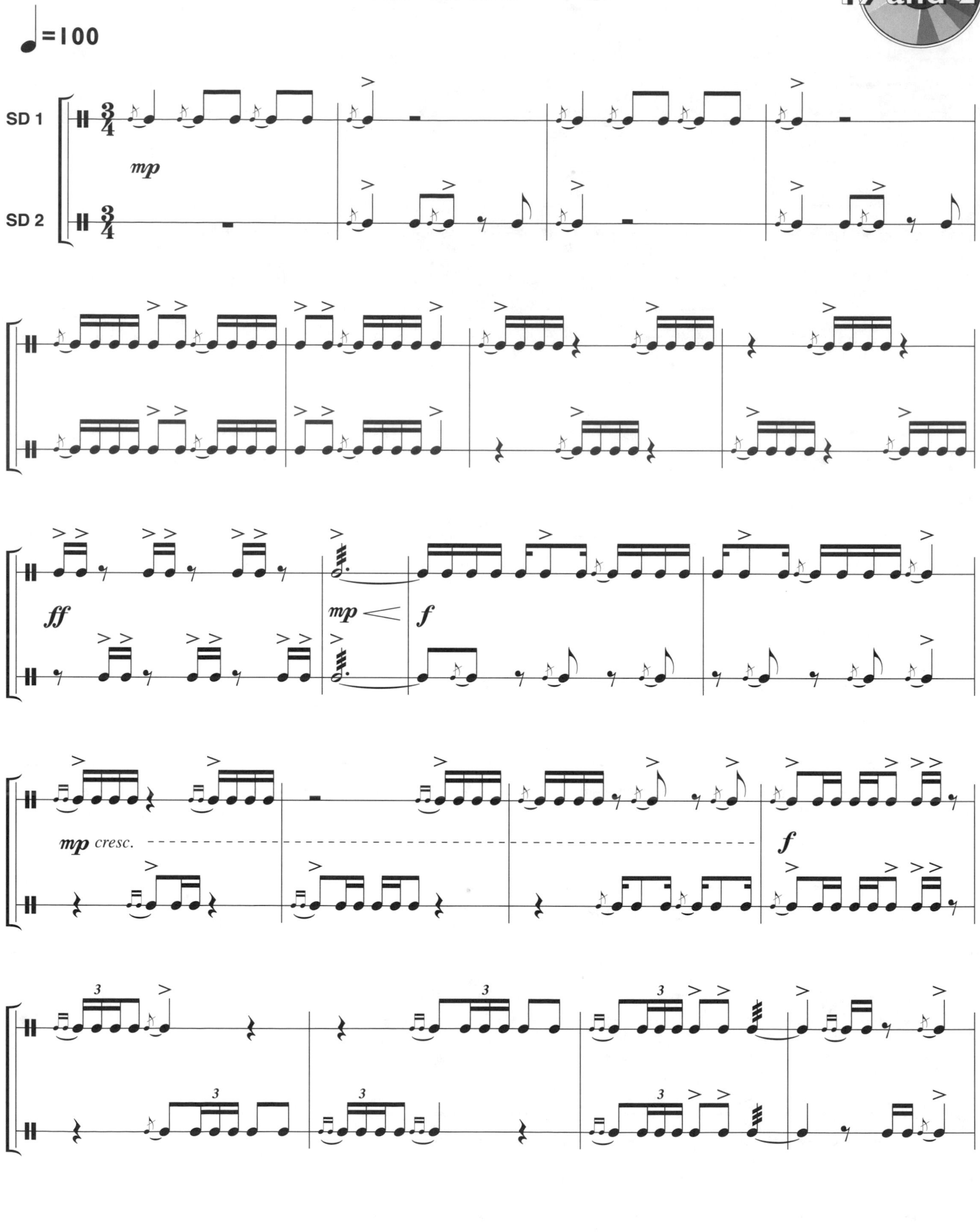

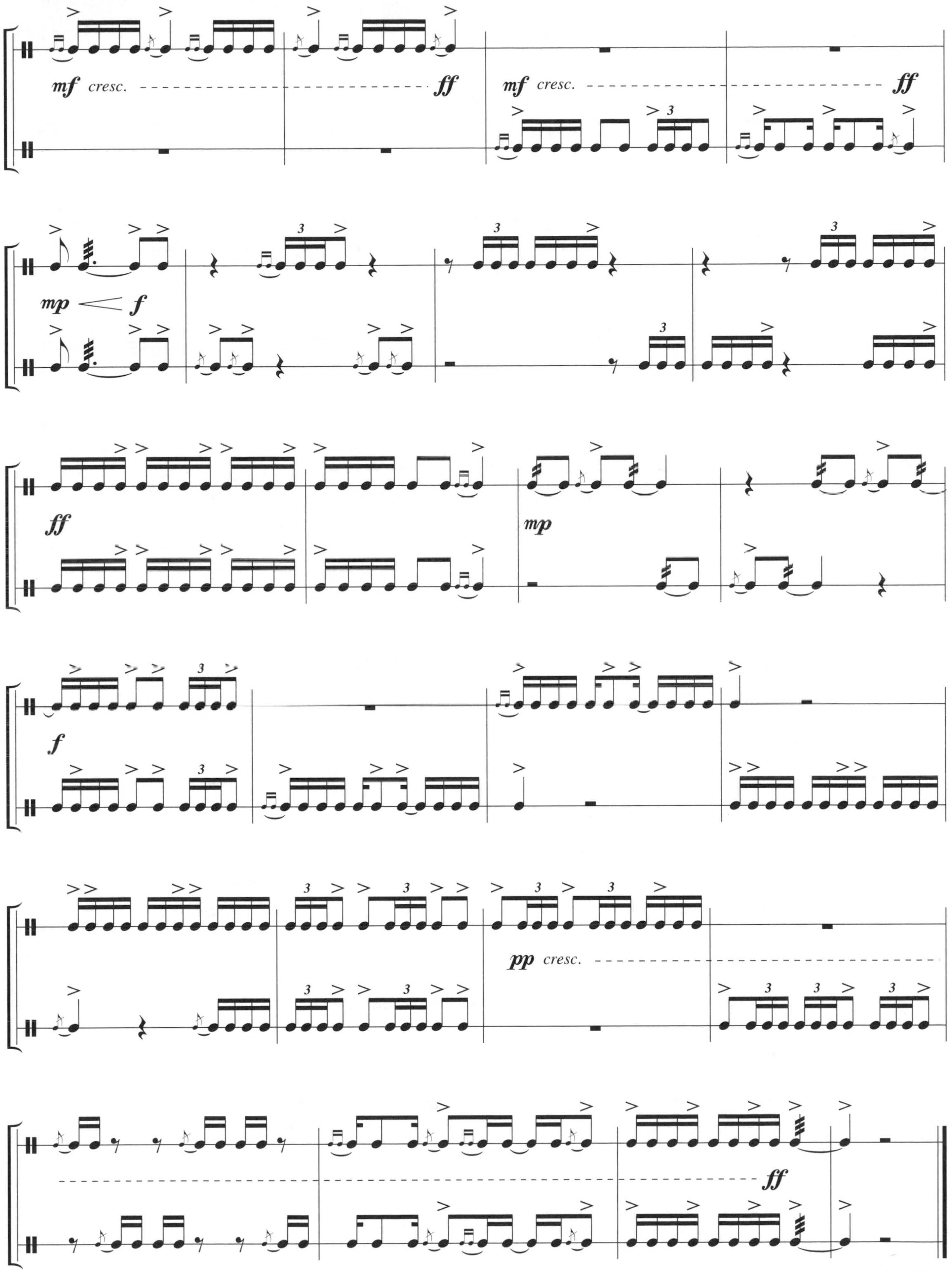
mf cresc.
ff
mf cresc.
ff
mp
f
ff
mp
f
pp cresc.
ff

Duet 11

Tracks 21 and 22

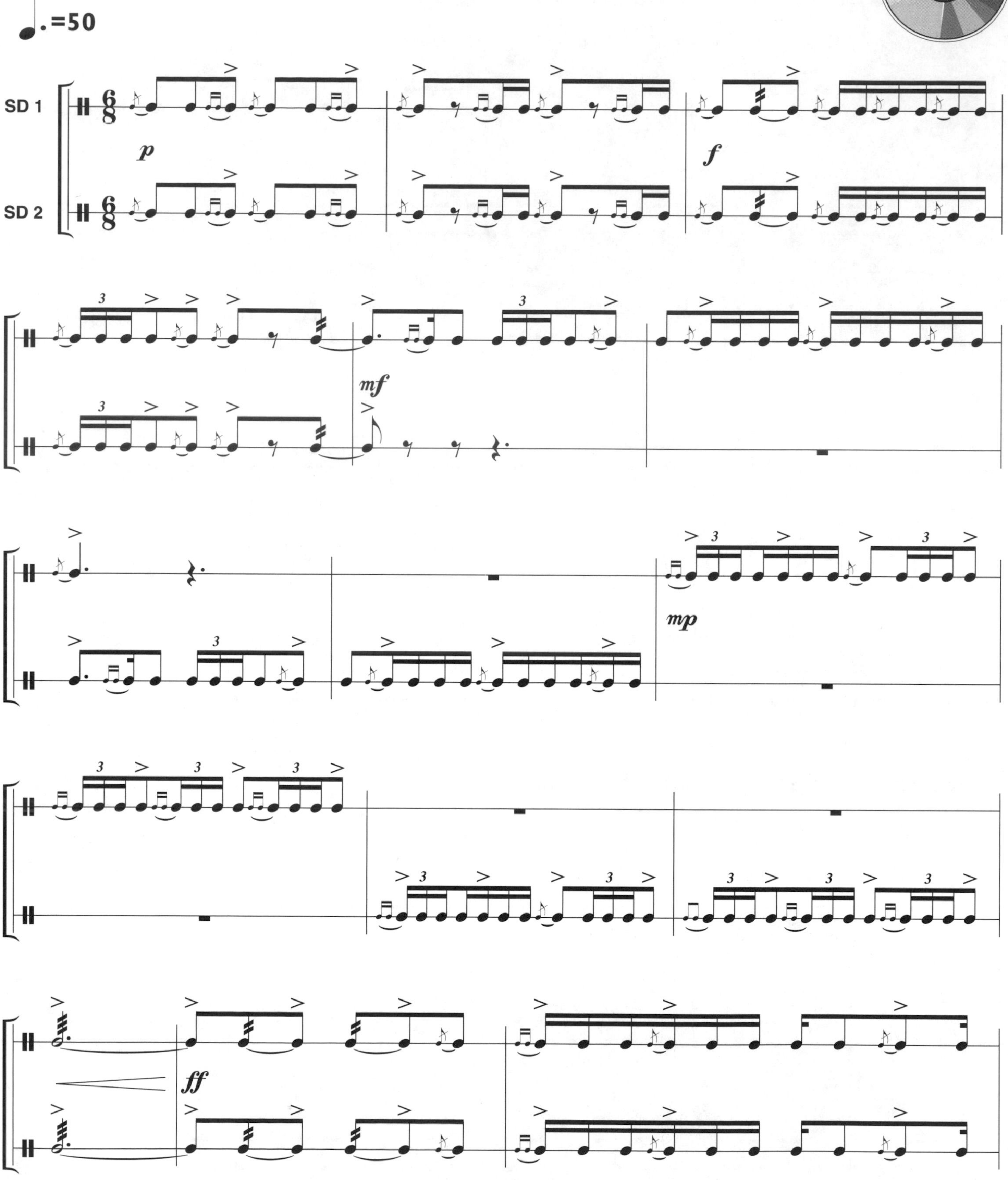

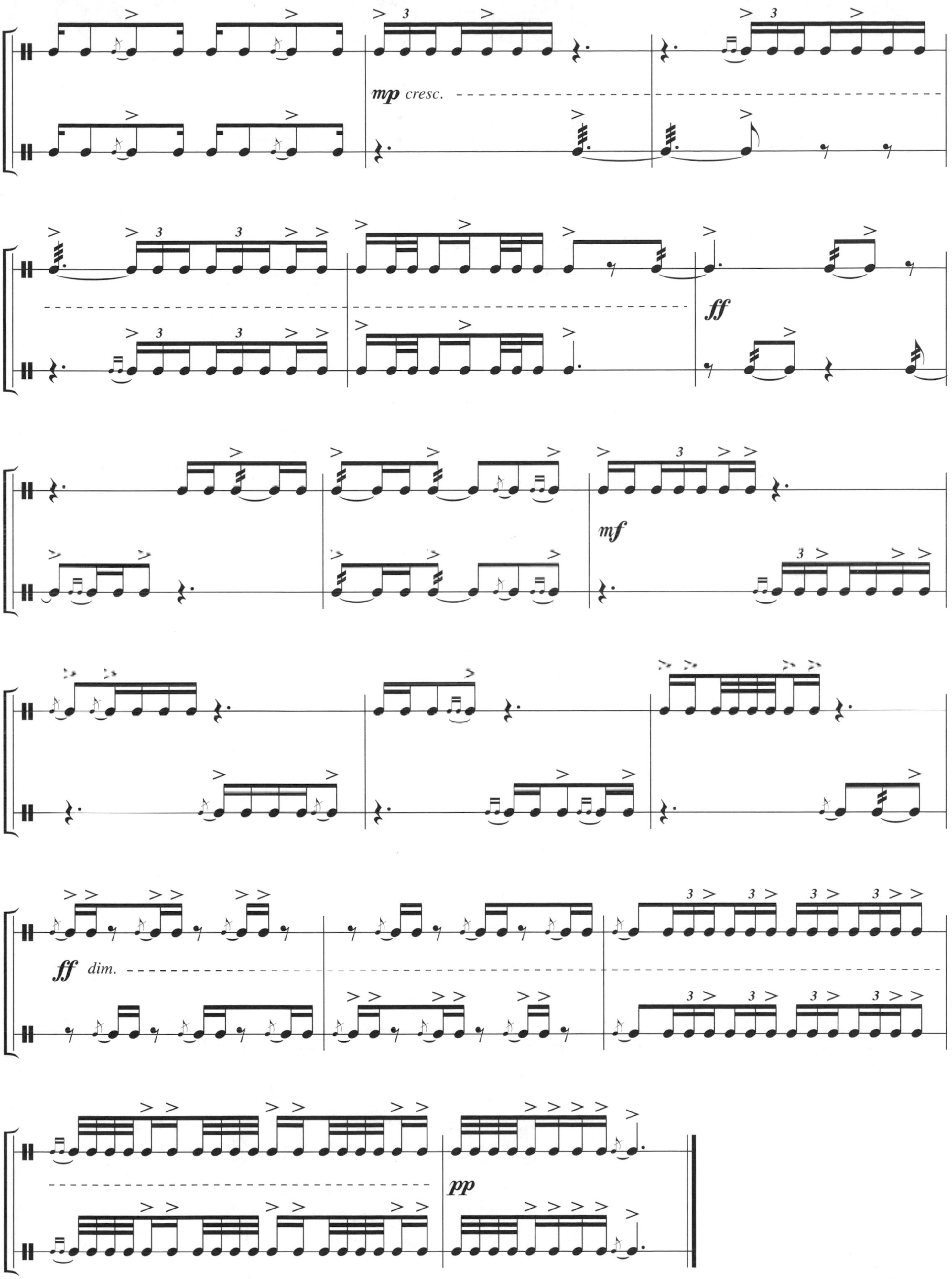
mp cresc.
ff
mf
ff dim.
pp

Duet 12

Tracks 23 and 24

♩ =79

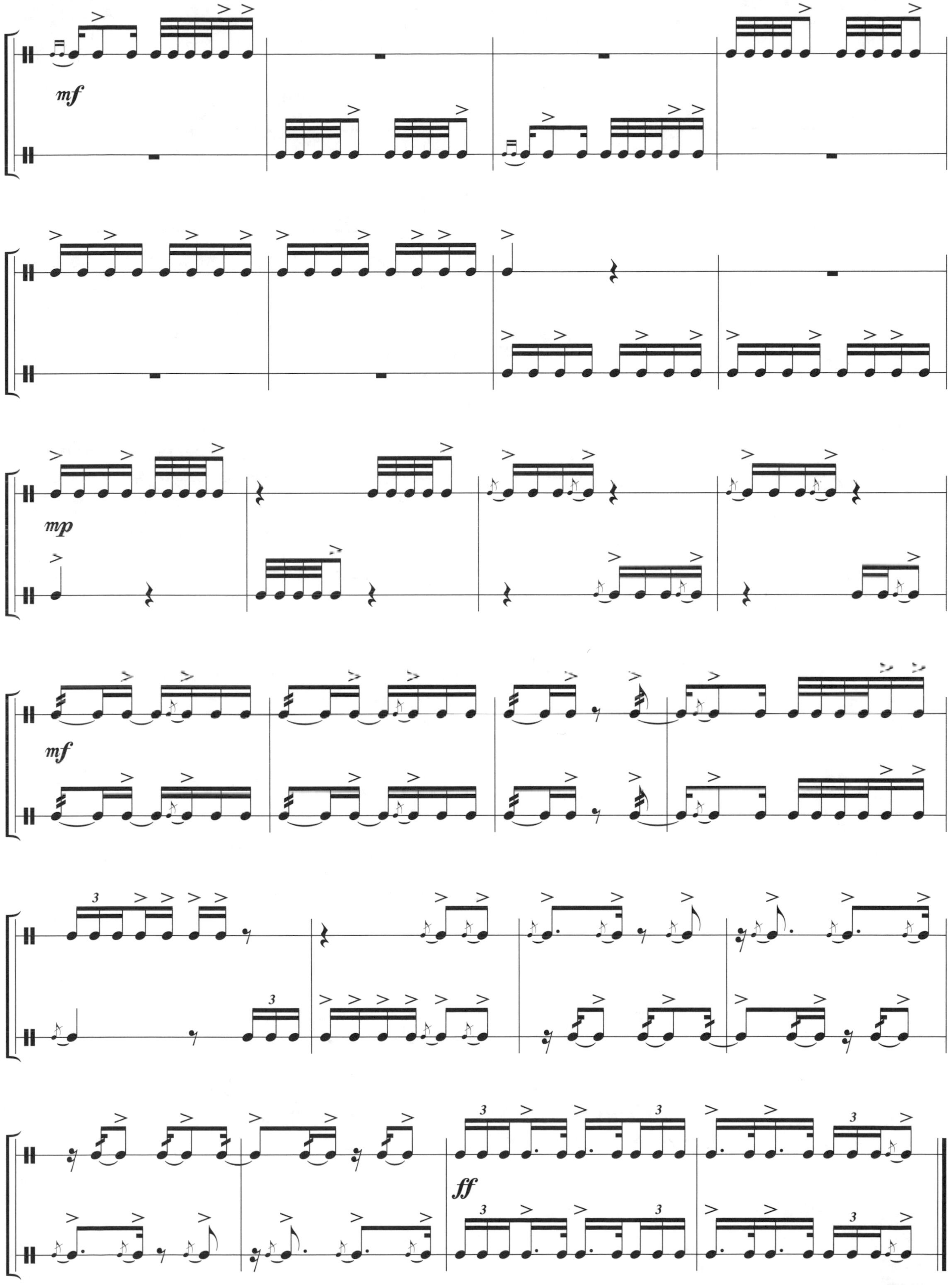
mf
mp
mf
3
3
3
3
3
3
3
3
ff

Duet 13

Tracks 25 and 26

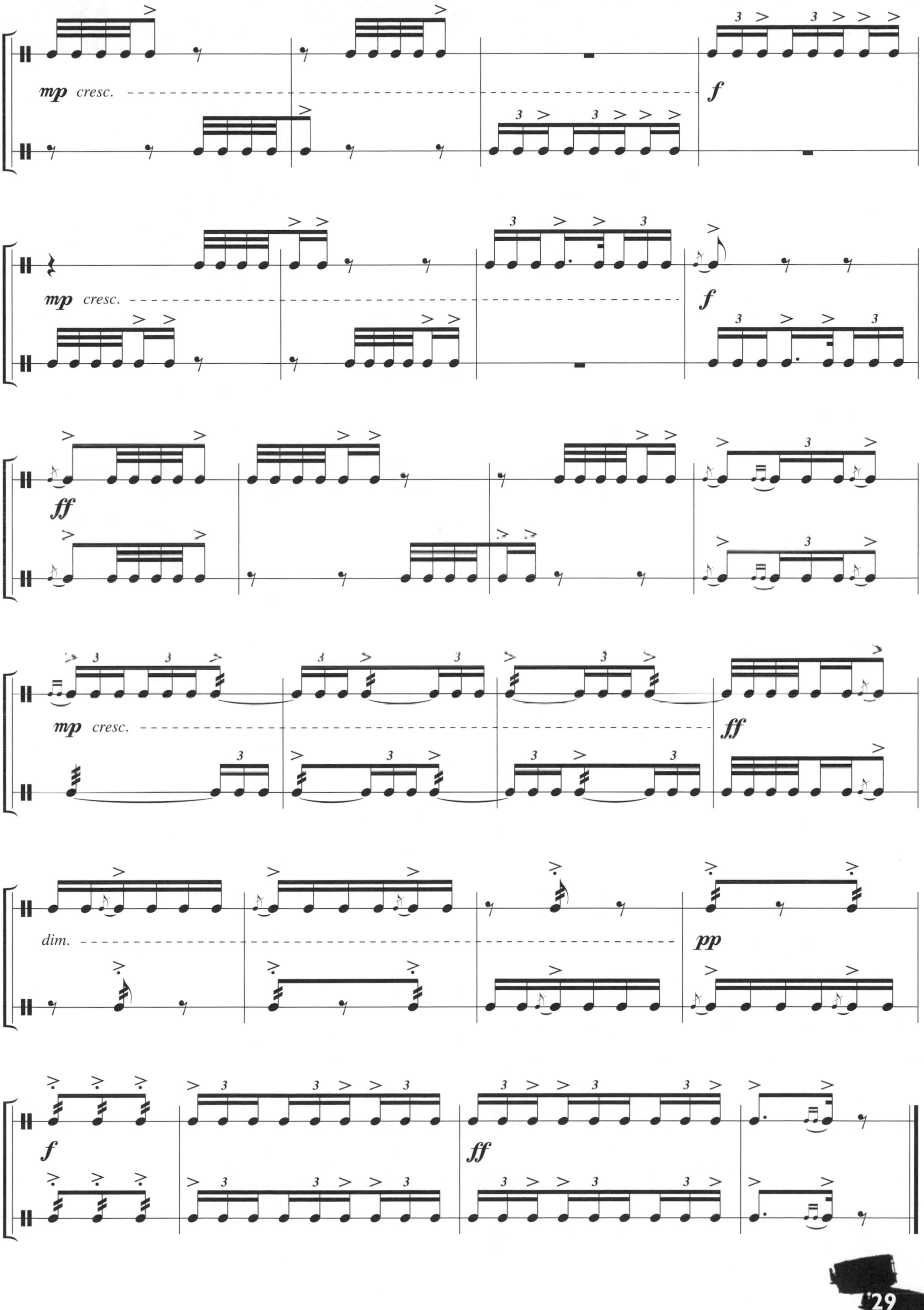
mp cresc.
f
mp cresc.
f
ff
mp cresc.
ff
dim.
pp
f
ff

Duet 14

Tracks 27 and 28

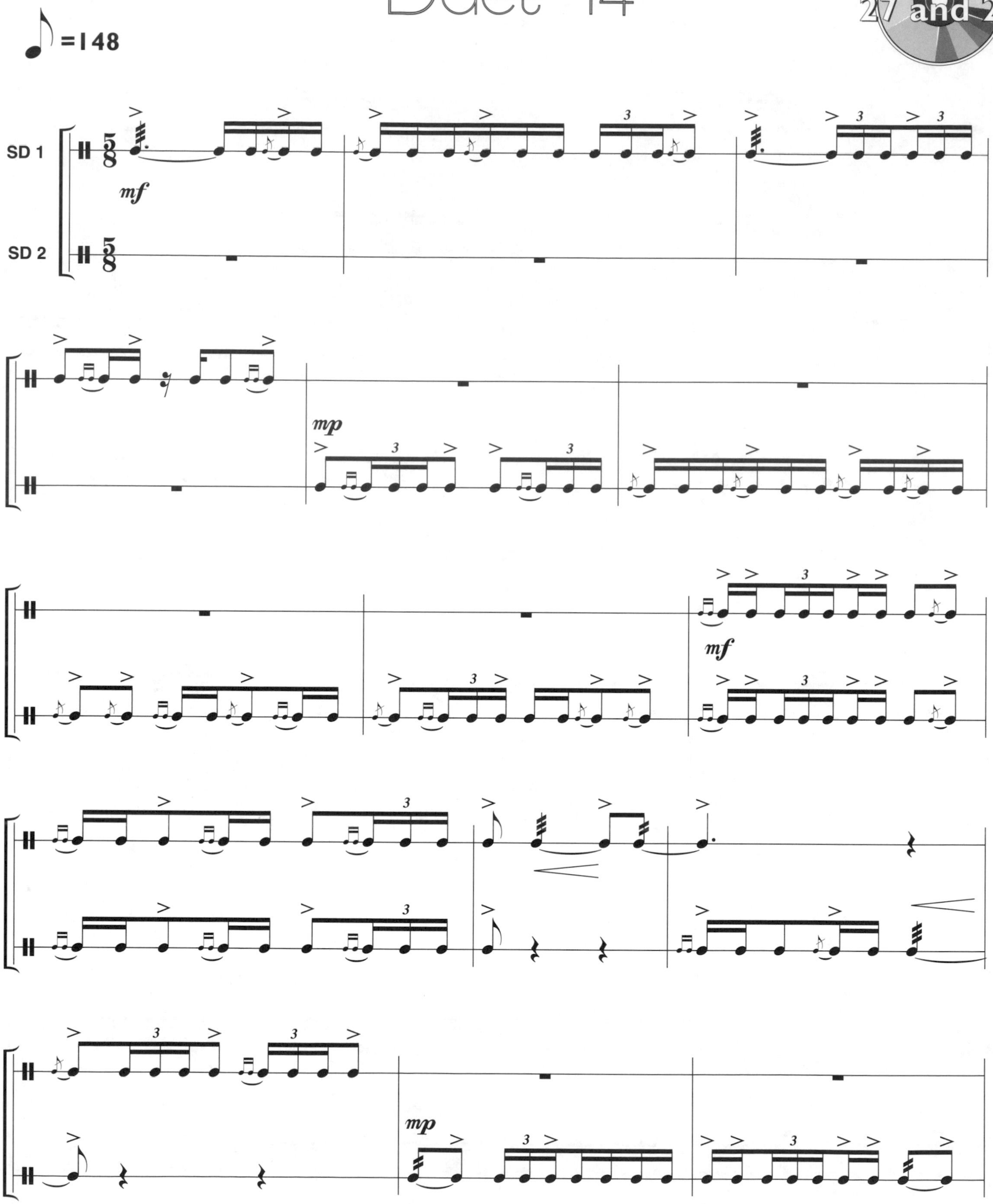

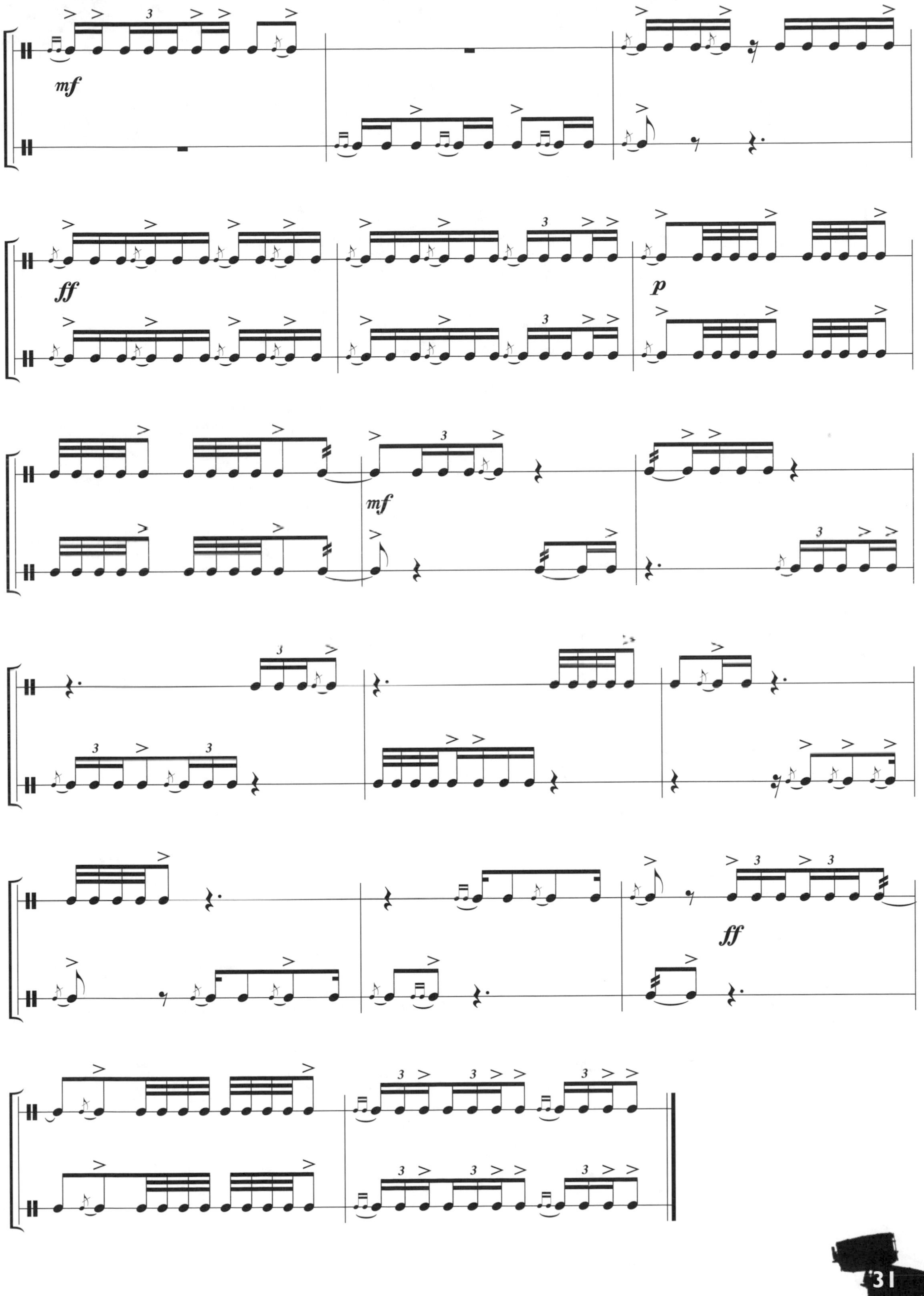
mf
ff
p
mf
ff

Duet 15

Tracks 29 and 30

♩=80

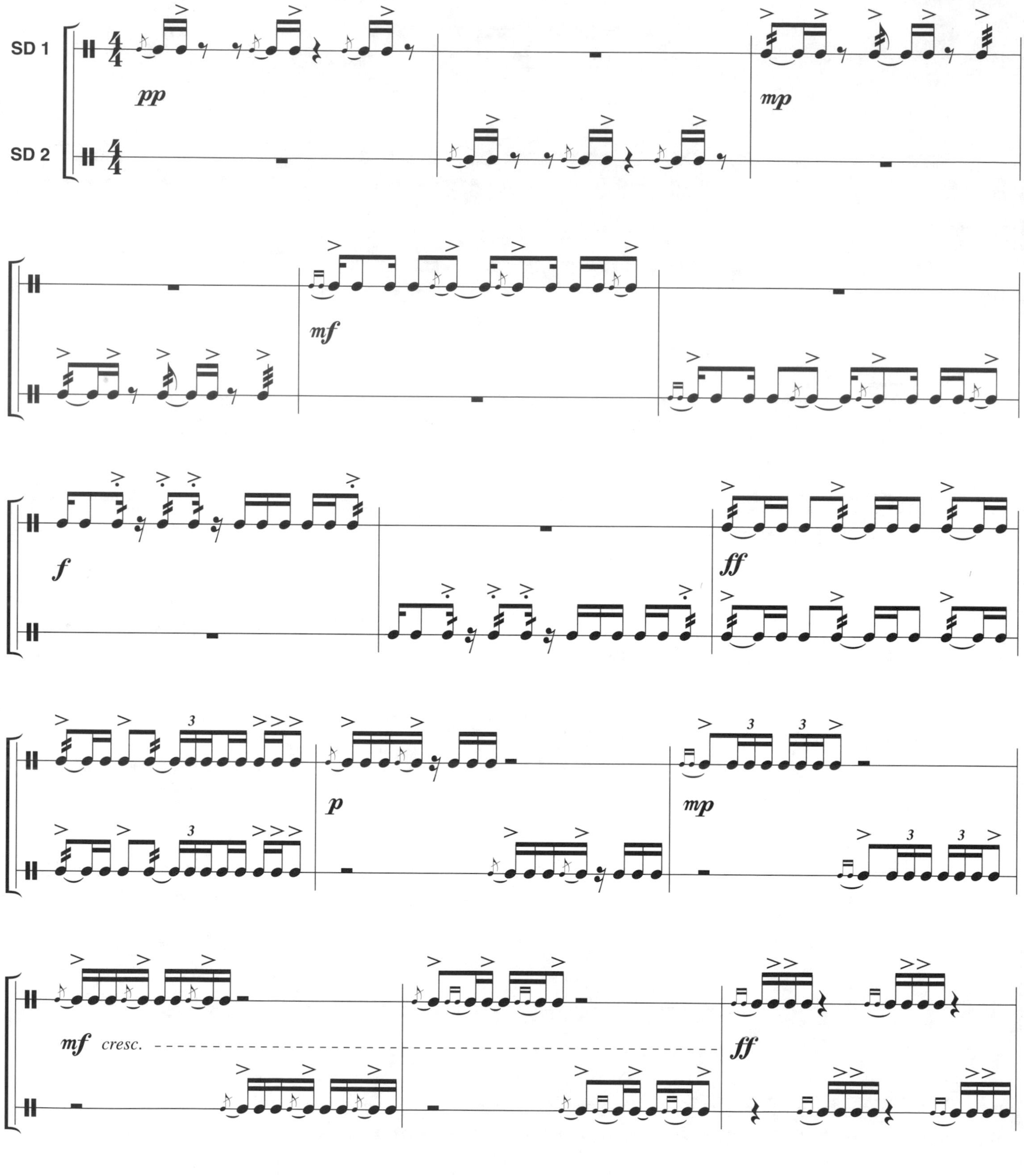

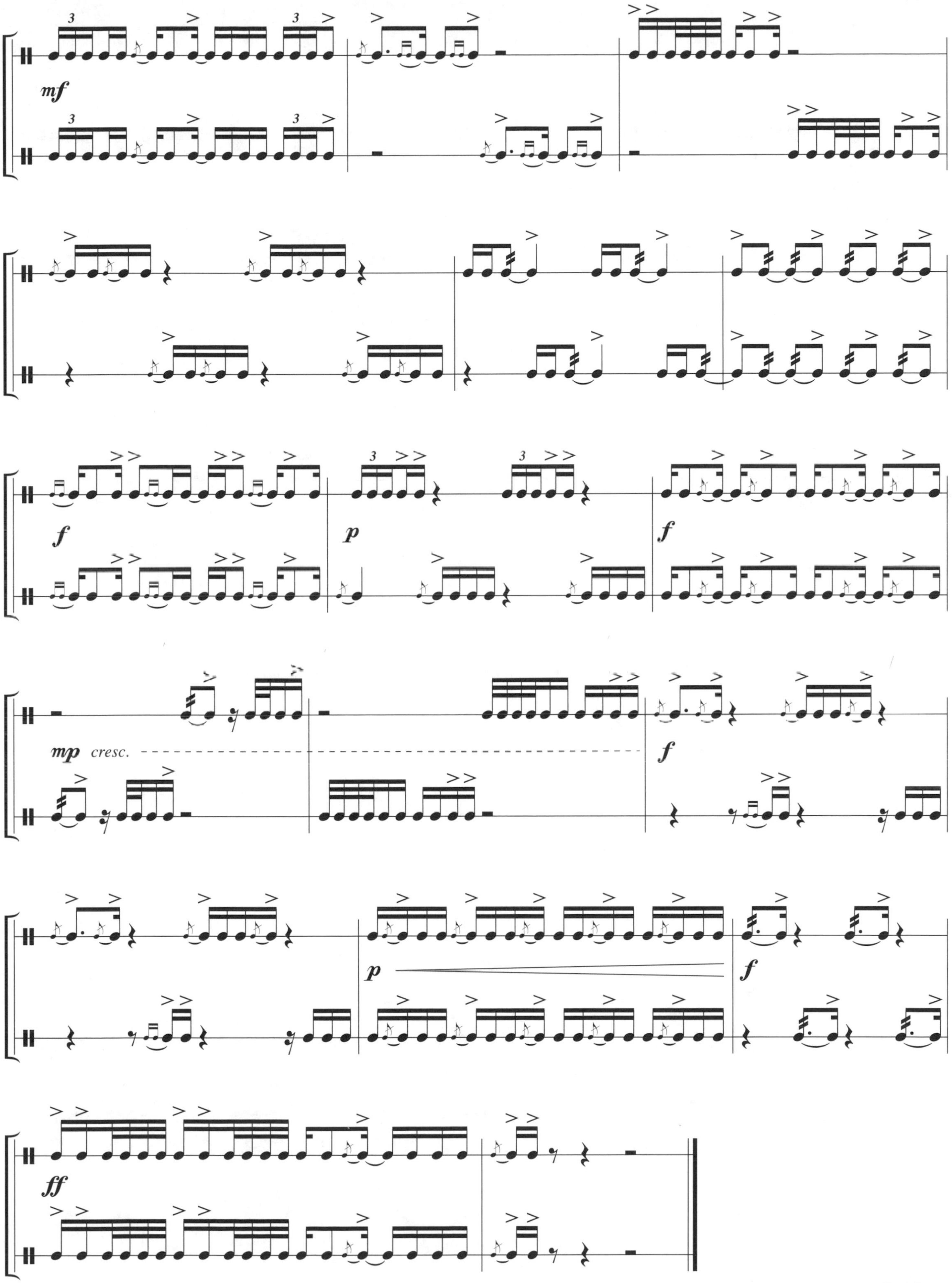
mf
f
p
f
mp cresc.
f
p
f
ff

Duet 16

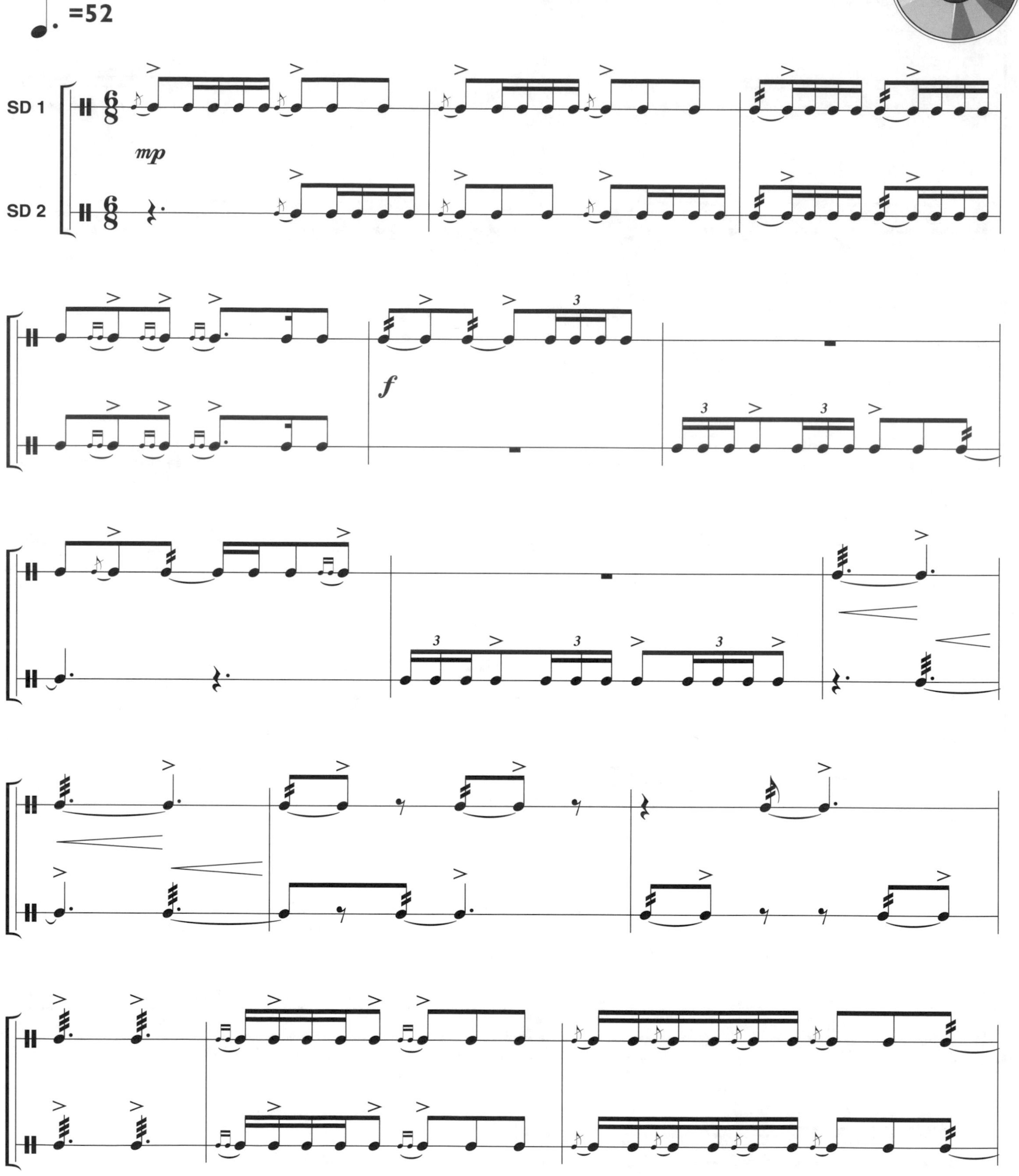

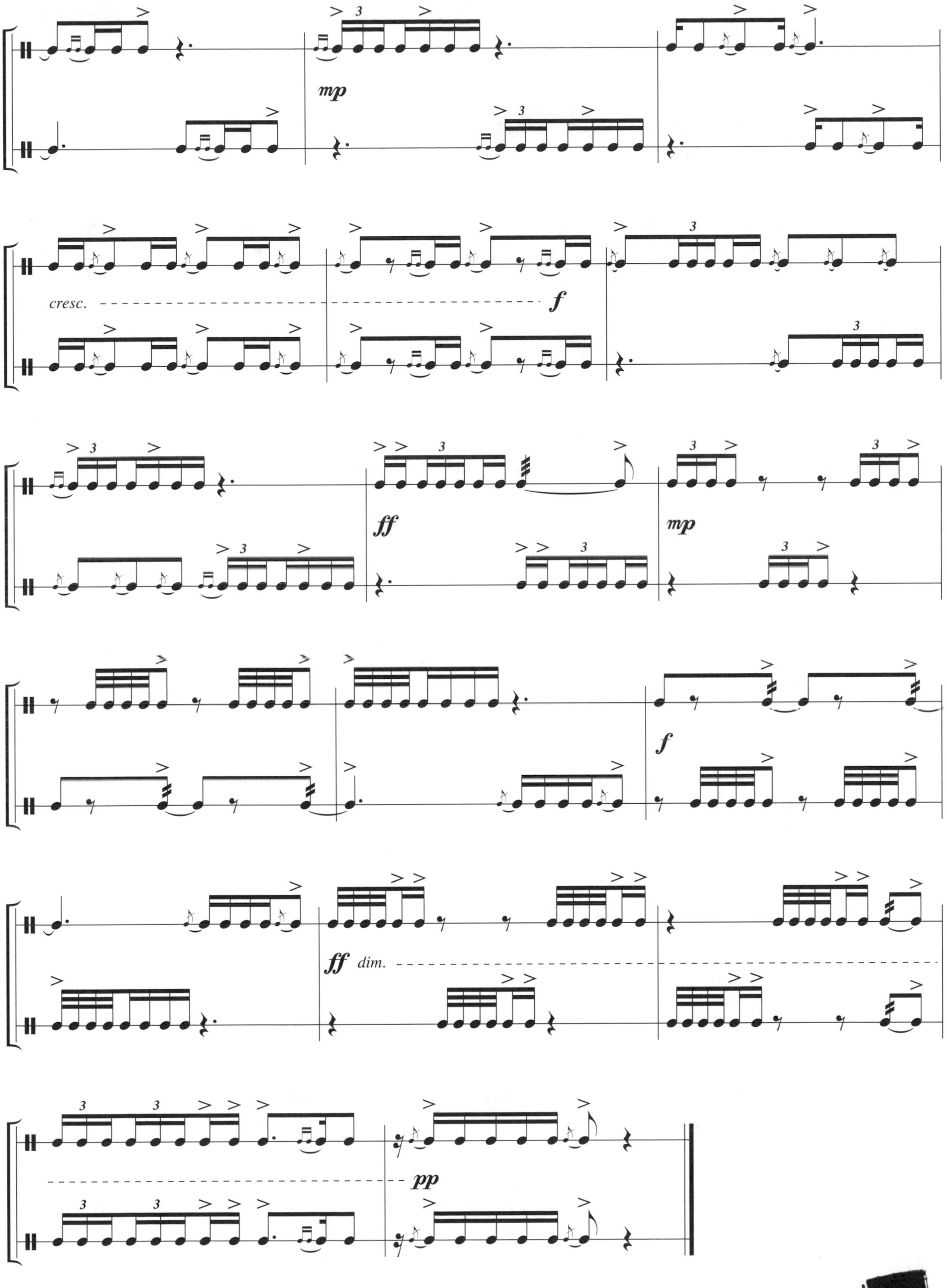
mp
cresc.
f
ff
mp
f
ff dim.
pp

Duet 17

Tracks 33 and 34

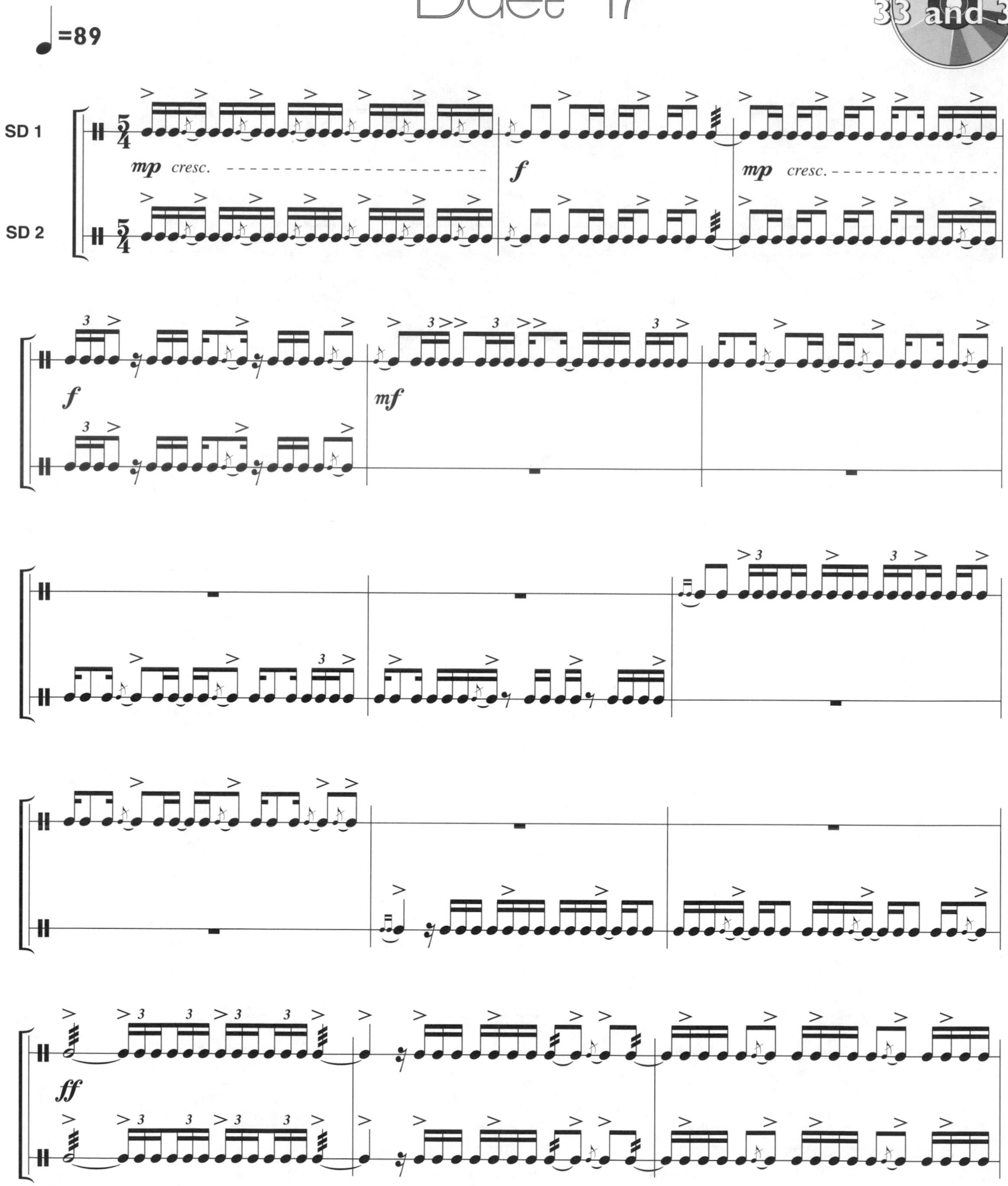

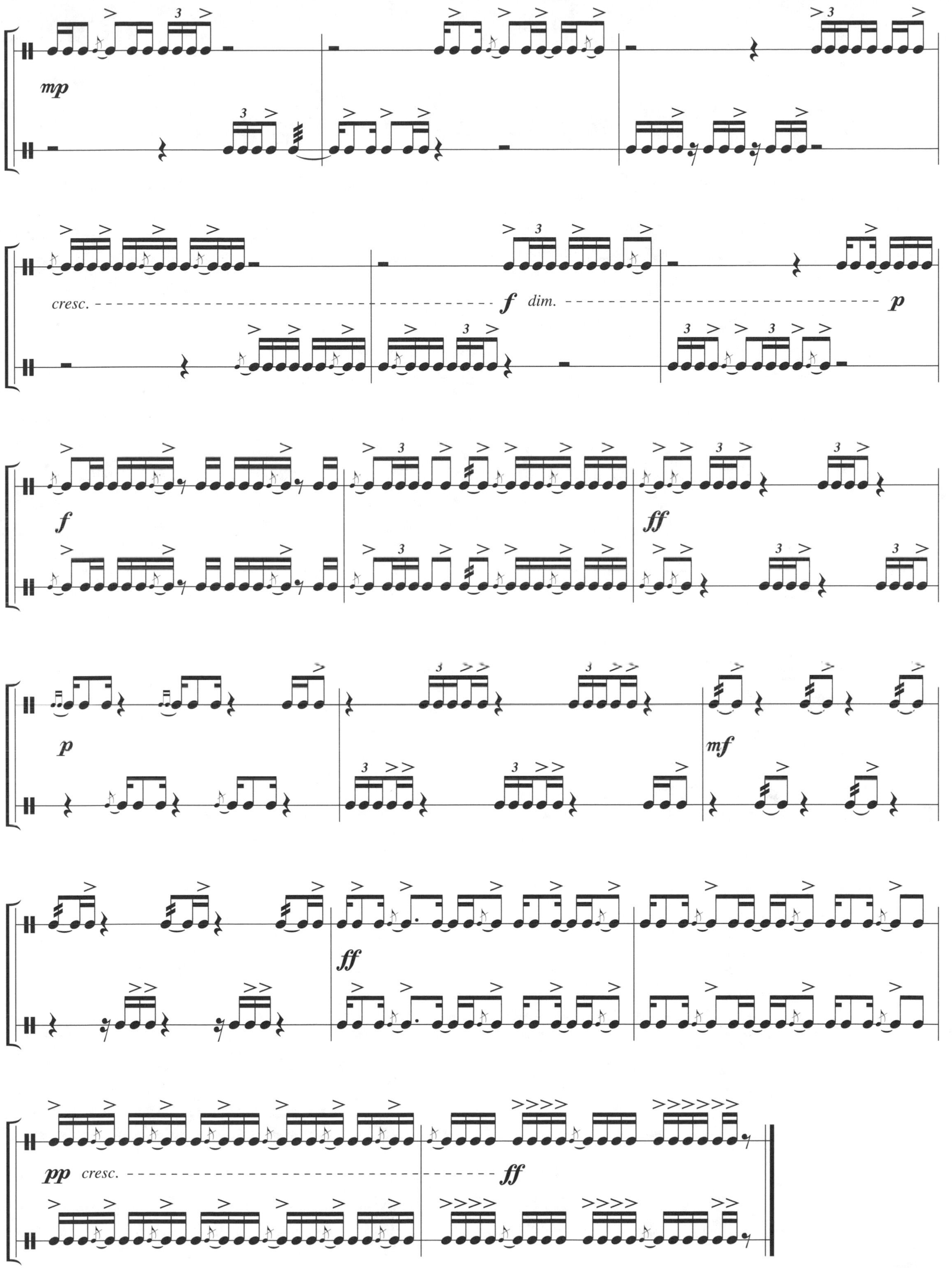
mp
cresc.
f
dim.
p
f
ff
p
mf
ff
pp
cresc.
ff

Duet 18

Tracks 35 and 36

♪ =166

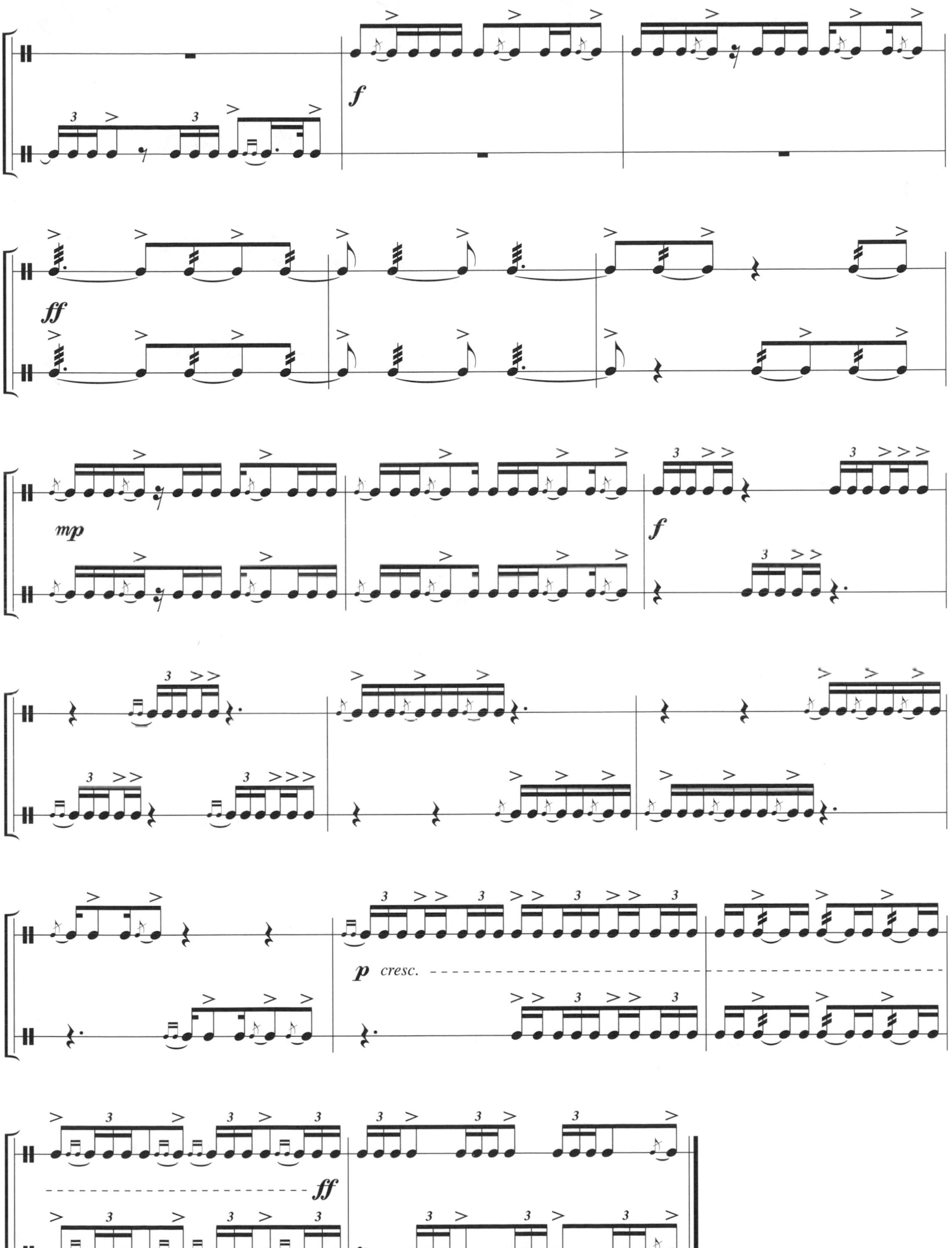
f
ff
mp
f
p cresc.
ff

Duet 19

Tracks 37 and 38

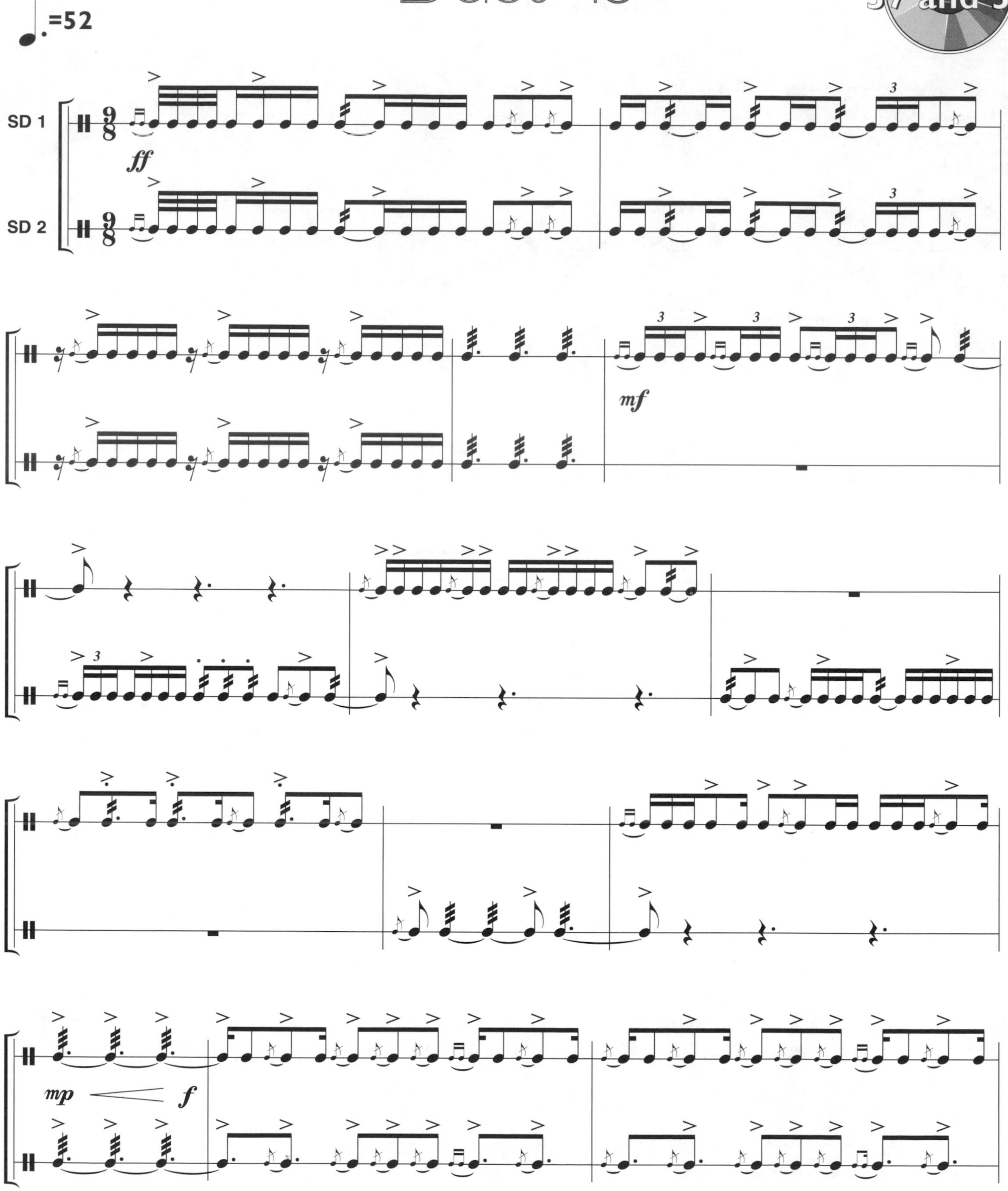

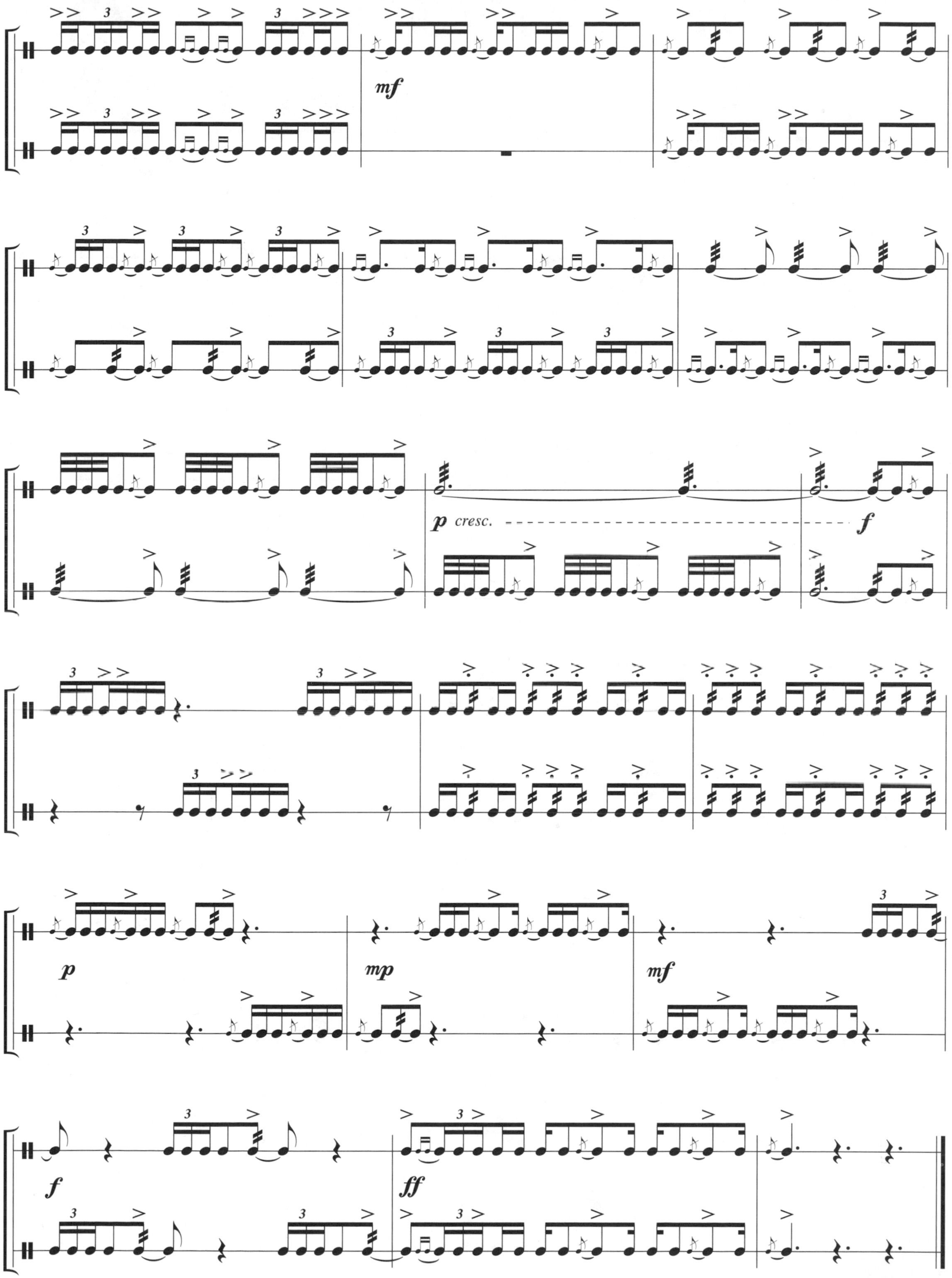
mf
p cresc.
f
p
mp
mf
f
ff

Duet 20

Tracks 39 and 40

♩=72

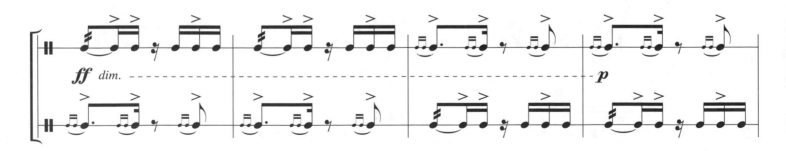

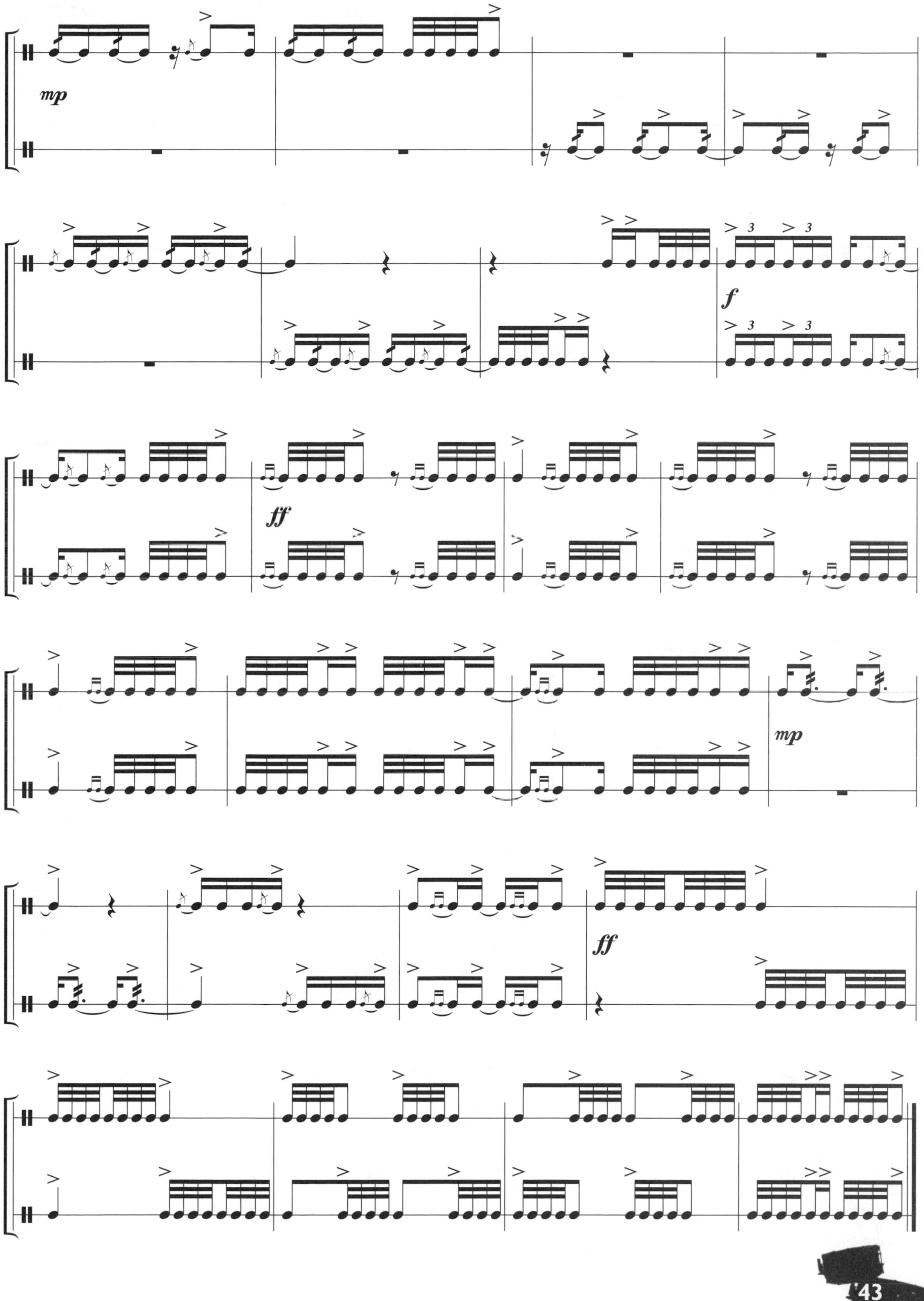
mp
f
ff
mp
ff

Duet 21

Tracks 41 and 42

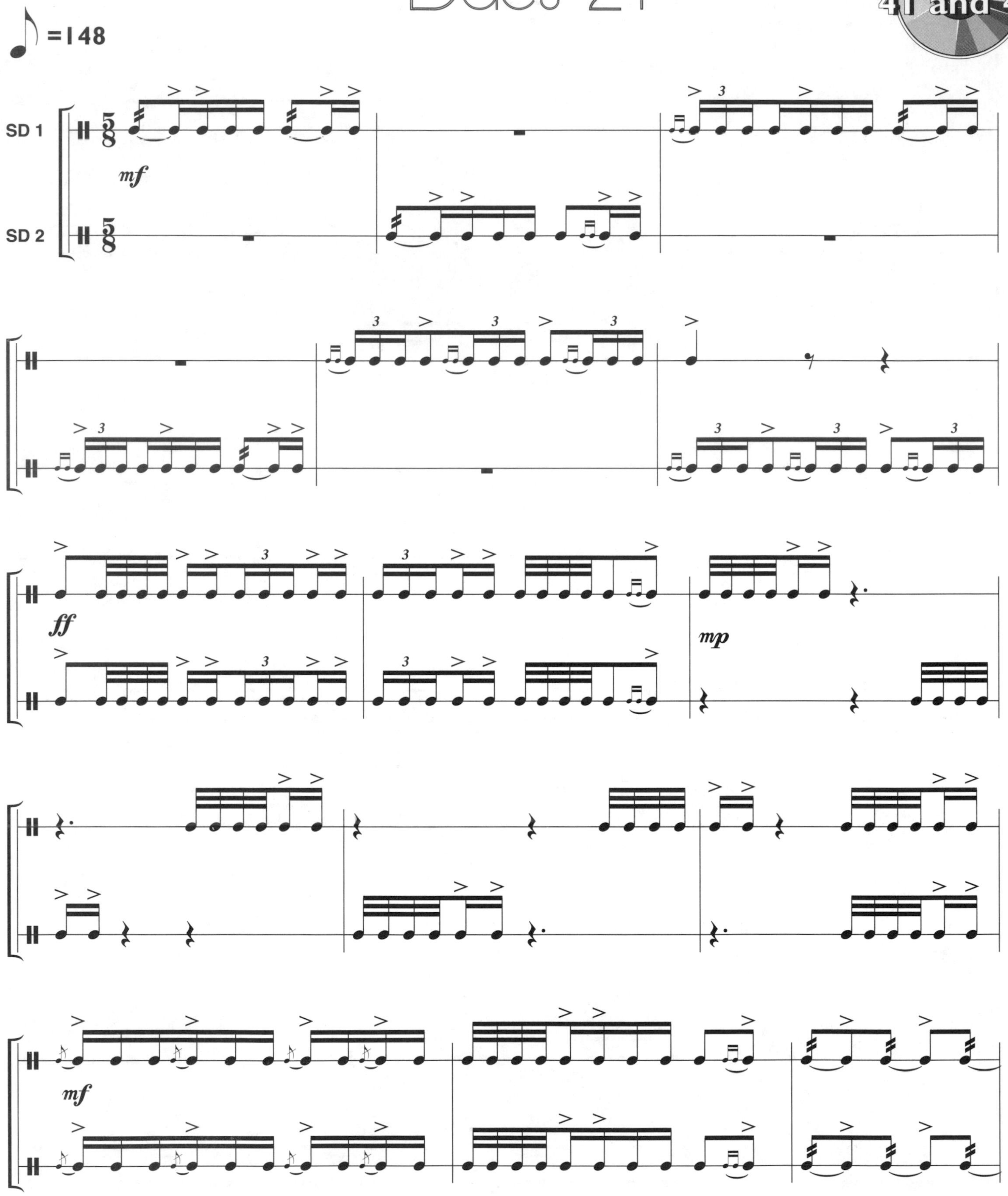

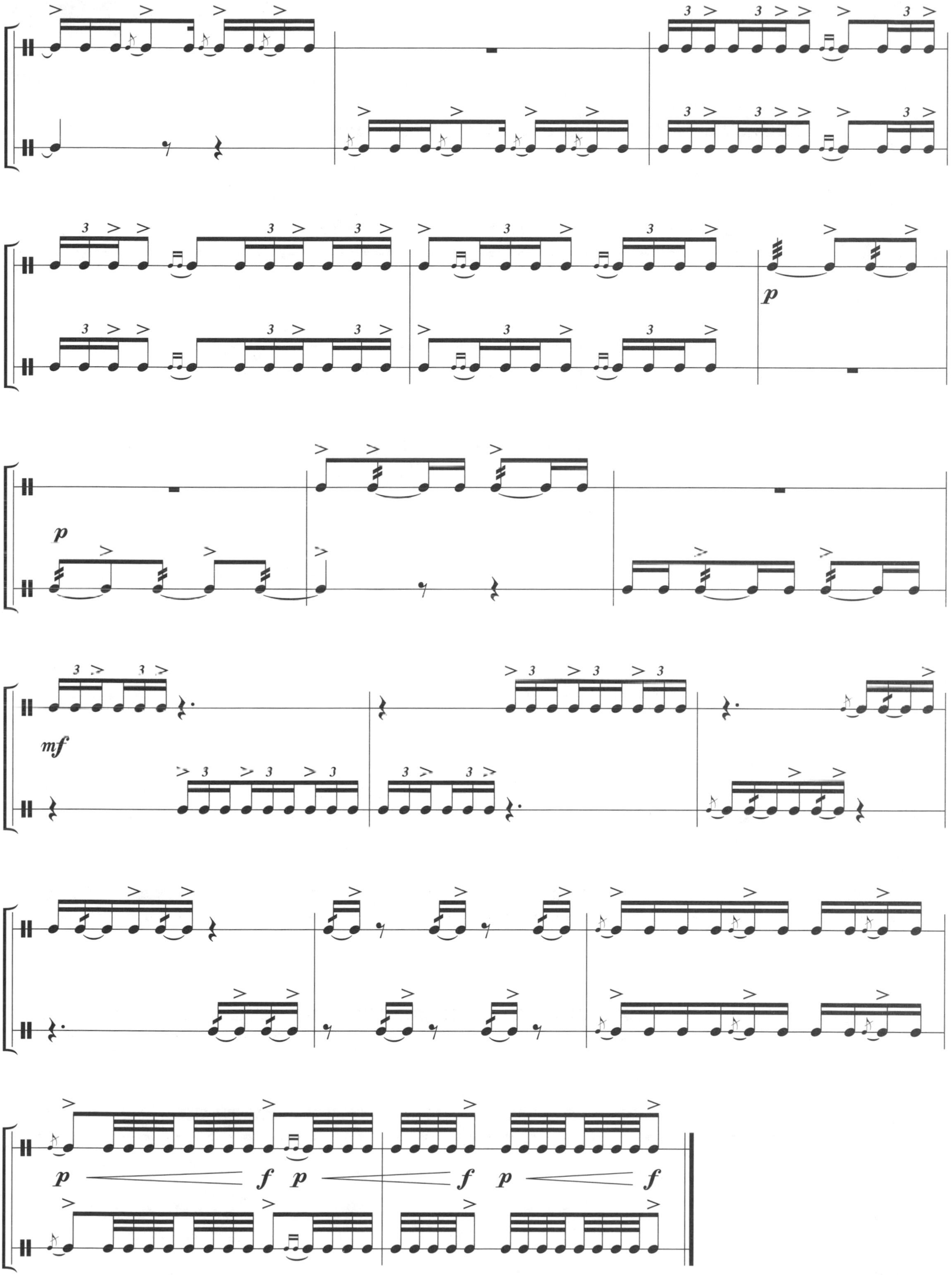

Duet 22

Tracks 43 and 44

♪=154

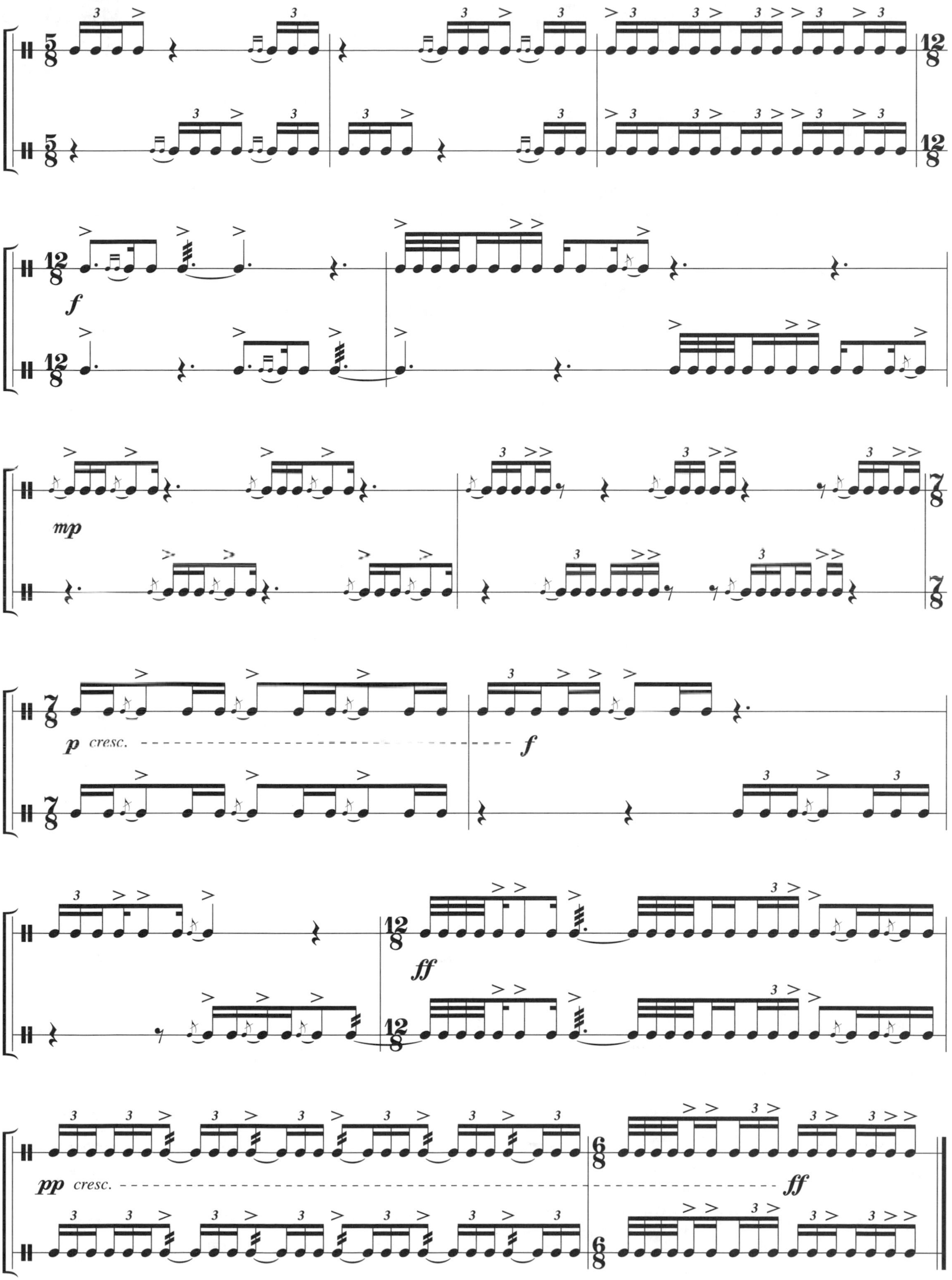
f
mp
p cresc.
f
ff
pp cresc.
ff

Duet 23

Tracks 45 and 46

♩. =50

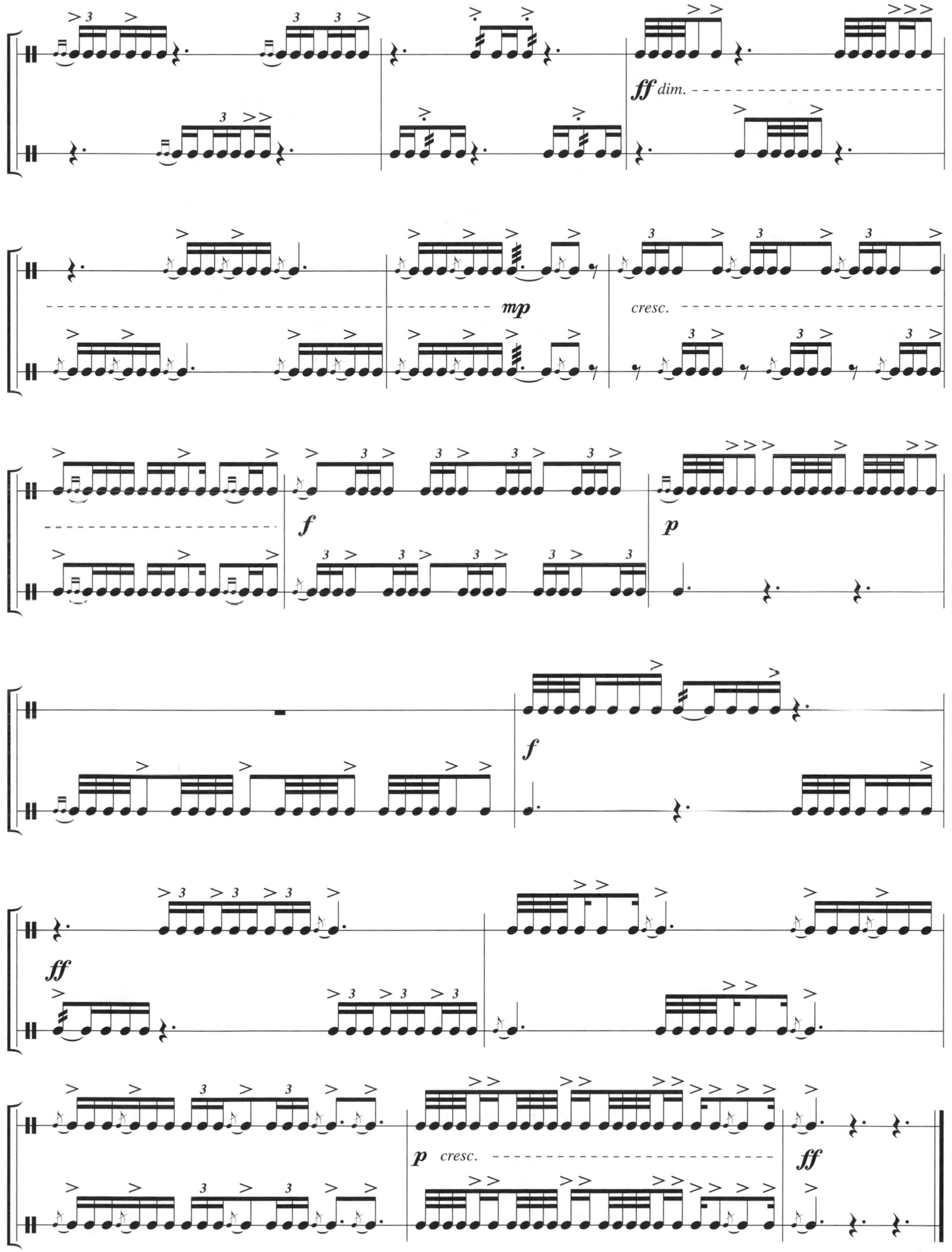
ff dim.
mp
cresc.
f
p
f
ff
p cresc.
ff

Tracks 47 and 48

Duet 24

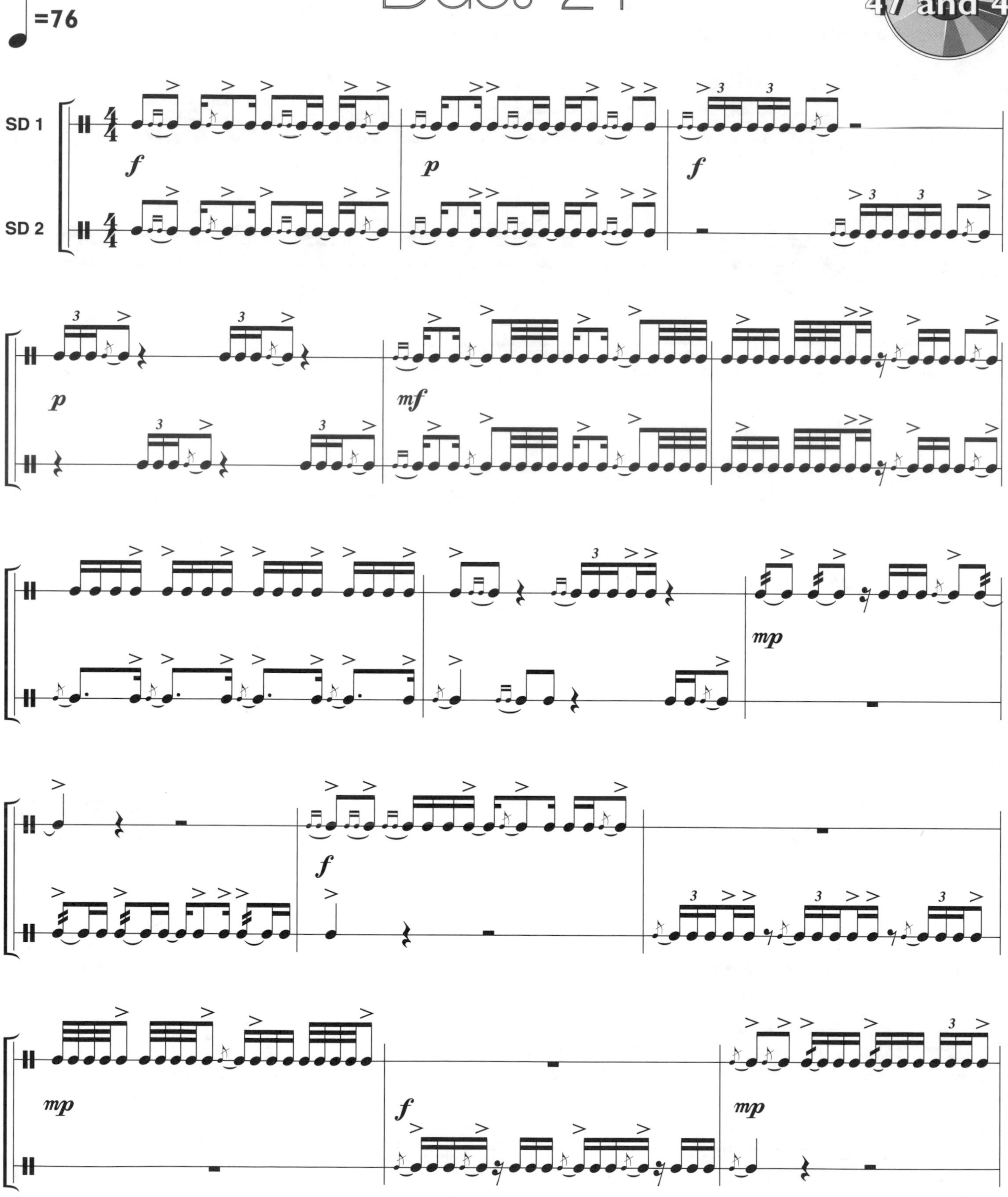

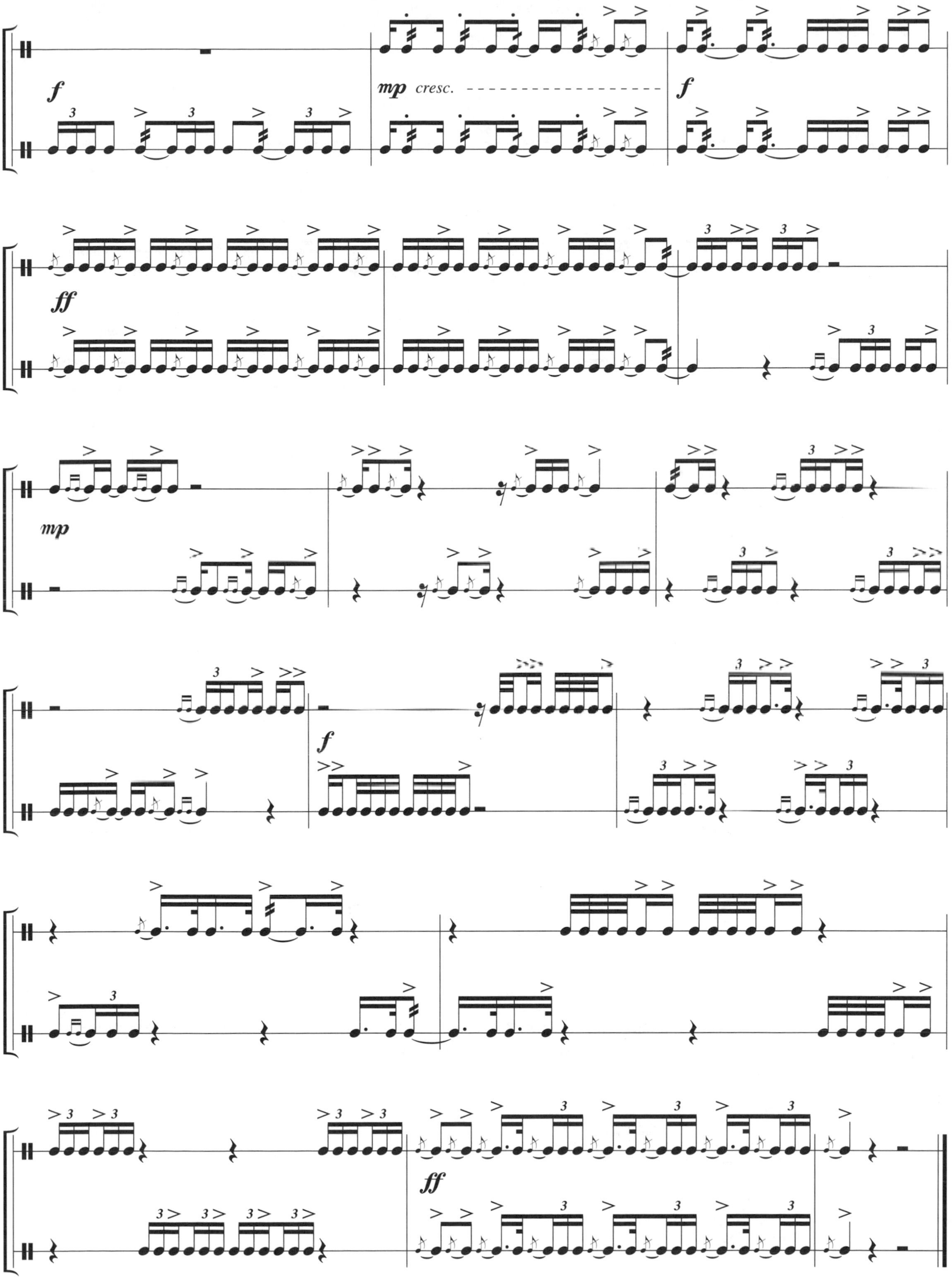
f
mp cresc.
f
ff
mp
f
ff

Duet 25

Tracks 49 and 50

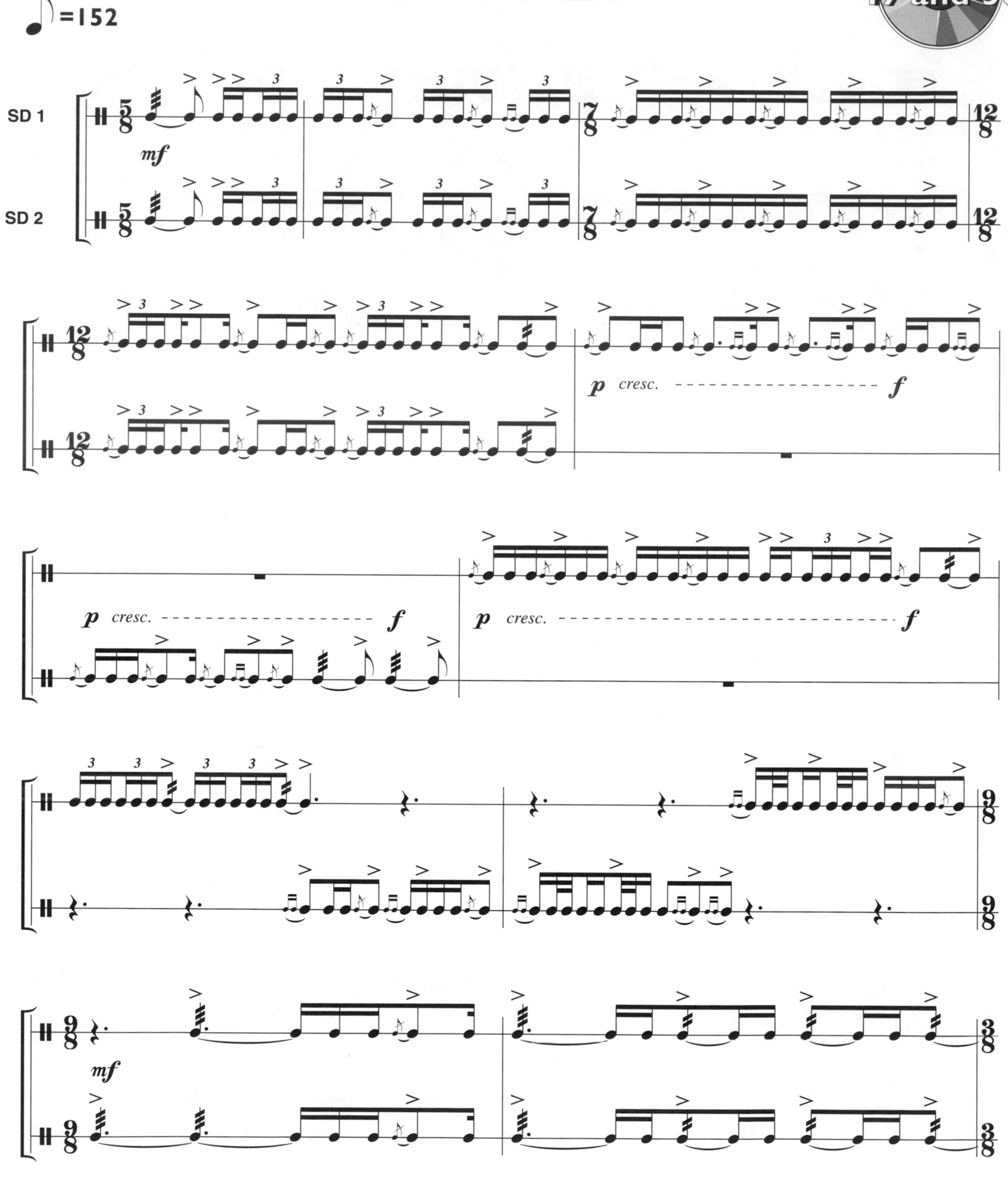

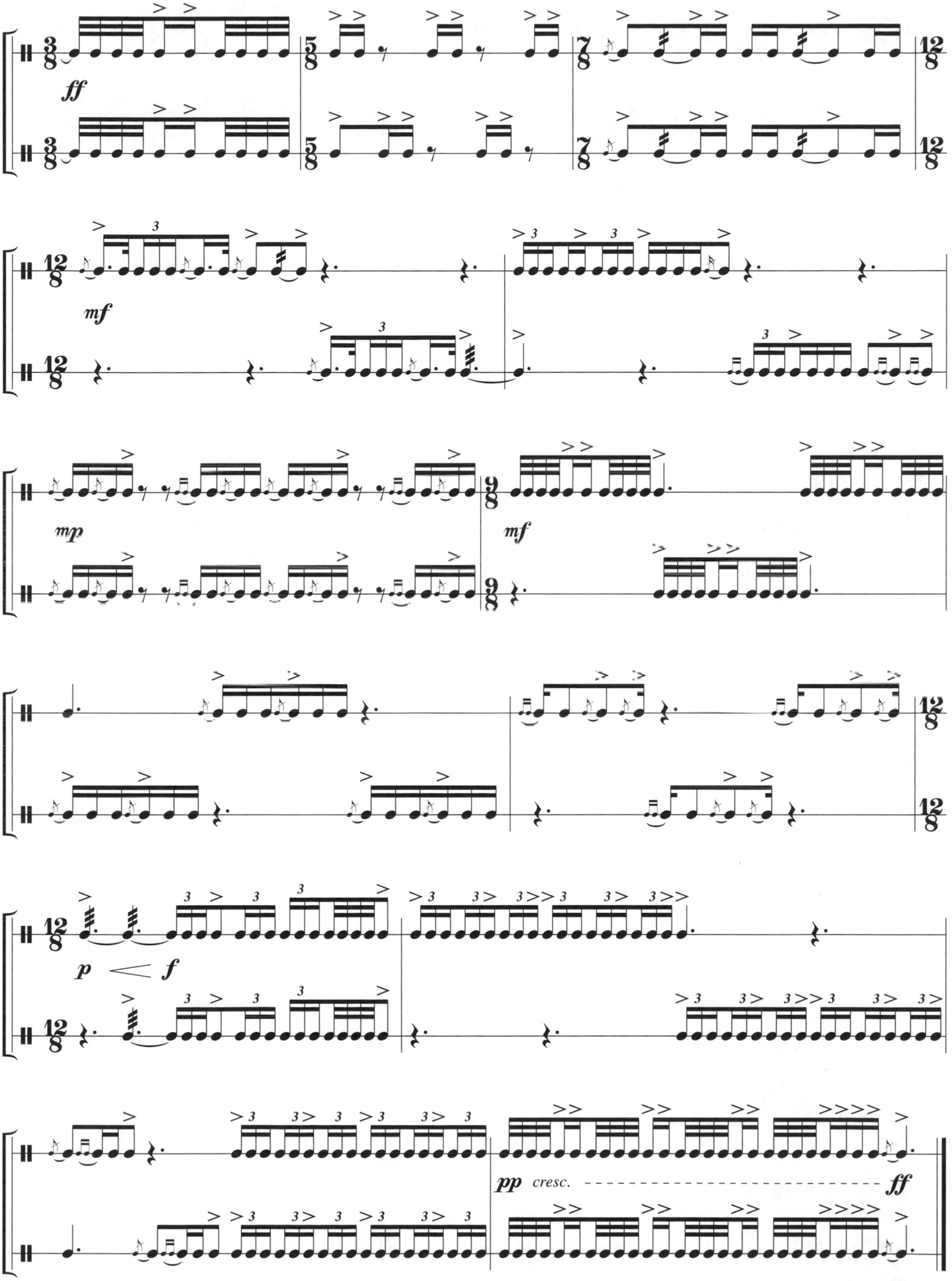
ff
mf
mp
mf
p
f
pp cresc.
ff

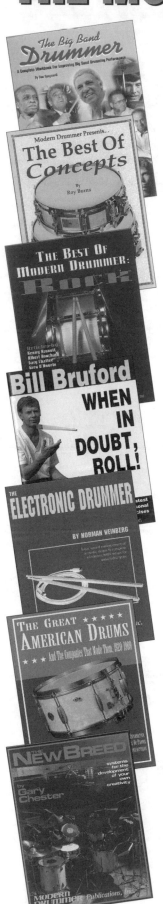

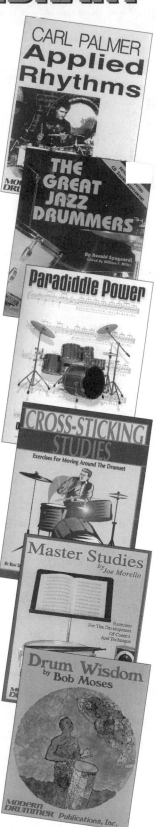

Drummers...

The Drummer's Studio Survival Guide
by Mark Parsons
The definitive book on recording drums, for the novice to professional drummer.

The Working Drummer
by Rick Van Horn
Everything the working clubdate drummer needs to know to succeed.

The Drummer's Time
by Rick Mattingly
A compilation of enlightening conversations with the great drummers of jazz, from Louie Bellson to Tony Williams.

Progressive Independence
by Ron Spagnardi
A comprehensive guide to coordinated independence for jazz drummers.

Progressive Independence: Rock
by Ron Spagnardi
163 pages of essential rock and funk drumming techniques.

The Modern Snare Drummer
by Ron Spagnardi
38 exciting snare drum solos that challenge reading and technical skills.

Double Bass Drumming
by Bobby Rondinelli & Michael Lauren
The most complete text on double bass ever written.

Name (please print) ______________________

Address ______________________

City ______________ State ______ Zip ______

❑ Payment Enclosed Charge: ❑ Visa ❑ MC ❑ Discover ❑ AmEx

Card # ______________ Exp Date ______

Signature ______________________

MAKE CHECK PAYABLE AND MAIL TO:
MUSIC DISPATCH
PO BOX 13920
MILWAUKEE, WI 53213

• ALL CHECKS OR MONEY ORDERS PAYABLE IN US FUNDS ONLY (NO CASH) •

Quantity	Book	Price	Total
	The Big Band Drummer (06620051)	$12.95	
	Applied Rhythms (06630365)	$8.95	
	The Best Of Concepts (06621766)	$9.95	
	The Great Jazz Drummers (06621755)	$19.95	
	The Best Of MD: Rock (06621759)	$9.95	
	Paradiddle Power (06620034)	$14.95	
	When In Doubt, Roll (06630298)	$13.95	
	Cross-Sticking Studies (00330377)	$12.95	
	The Electronic Drummer (06631500)	$9.95	
	Master Studies (06631474)	$12.95	
	The Great American Drums (06620010)	$19.95	
	Drum Wisdom (06630510)	$7.95	
	The New Breed (06631619)	$12.95	
	Studio Survival Guide (00330257)	$12.95	
	The Working Drummer (00330264)	$14.95	
	The Drummer's Time (00330454)	$12.95	
	Progressive Independence (00330290)	$12.95	
	Progressive Independence Rock (06620049)	$14.95	
	The Modern Snare Drummer (00330458)	$12.95	
	Double Bass Drumming (06620037)	$12.95	

SHIPPING AND HANDLING CHARGES (See box below) ______

Minnesota and Wisconsin residents add appropriate sales tax. ______

GRAND TOTAL ______

SHIPPING AND HANDLING
up to $25.99: add $4.50
$26.00 – $40.99: add $5.50
$41.00 and up: add $6.50

MOD19

ORDER TOLL-FREE
(800) 637-2852
M-F: 9AM–8PM, SAT 9AM–2PM CST

OR ONLINE AT
www.moderndrummer.com

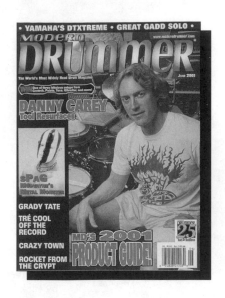

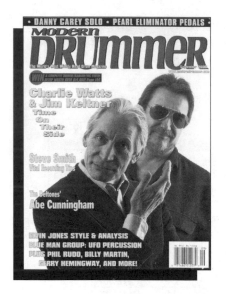